THAT PICTURE (

Susan J Bevan

SUSAN J BEVAN

This book is dedicated to all the birth mothers throughout the world who have lived in the hope that one day they may meet their child again.

SUSAN J BEVAN

ACKNOWLEDGEMENT

I would like to take this opportunity to thank all my family for the support they have provided in this turbulent journey from 15-year-old birth mother to 56-year-old author. Without them this book would not exist. I'd like too to thank all those friends along the way who insisted I am a writer and should write this remarkable story. I hope they enjoy reading the fruits of their encouragement. And I would like to share this book with all the birth mothers out there. It is estimated that more than half a million women in the UK have lost their children to adoption. I hope this story helps just some of them in their healing. But most of all I would like to thank Ben for showing me what a wonderful experience mothering for life can be, and Bert for helping co-create him. For Helen and her two beautiful children of her own, I hope this book answers some of your questions. I wish you love, and arms to hold you.

SUSAN J BEVAN

CONTENTS

THAT PICTURE OF YOU

SUSAN J BEVAN

Prologue

"I think you'd better sit down."

Somehow I've managed to reach the age of thirty-seven without anyone ever having said that to me. Until now. The words hang in the air like little beads of toxic cloud, waiting to release their poison. Even when I was told my father had dropped dead of a sudden unexpected heart attack, I'd been allowed to stay on my feet. It had taken only a moment though for me to collapse in the corner of a foreign sofa far from home, emitting a visceral guttural wail I'd only heard in films. I was nineteen. My father had been a tender forty-nine.

The night I lost my dad. New Year's Eve, and for the first time in my life I'd spent it away from home, in Trafalgar Square celebrating to the sounds of Big Ben with my wonderful boyfriend. One of the most exciting and liberating moments of my life. London! We'd drunk too much real ale (naturally) and danced around the Lutyens fountain with odd little fireworks going off around us, relishing beery kisses as midnight struck for us and a heart attack struck my father.

Then the official fireworks exploded a rainbow overhead like the Big Bang all over again – my own beginning of a brand new life. I was nineteen and in love - finally grown up. A new year, a new start, and so much living to do. I couldn't have been happier.

Meanwhile my father was home asleep and alone as a massive aneurism struck him in the bare spare bedroom of our Valleys semi, overlooking the pithead and the slag heap. His snoring had driven my mother mad for years. Separate beds were nothing new. She woke next morning to find him long dead. That was our New Year's morning 1976.

Should old acquaintance be forgot...

"I think you'd better sit down."

I need to. It's 1993. June. The day's been a long, hot one. Rehearsals from early morning, on a play I've both written and directed, are taking their toll on this heavily pregnant prima gravitas thirty-seven year old. Or at least, that's what most people thought I was – until I wrote this play. Autobiographical and raw, it tells the story of my fifteen-year-old self falling pregnant in Mountain Ash in the Welsh Valleys in the early seventies. Attitudes changed slowly in Mount: to get a feel for life there in the seventies, think conventional small town in the fifties.

The play, *Half A Million Women,* is mostly set there and tells the agonising tale of my teenage pregnancy, how I was sent away to give birth in secret some three hundred miles from home, and finally the forcible taking of my daughter for adoption at eight days.

Eight days – the only life I had with my child; a lifetime in the blinking of an eye. It seemed she was gone before I could even fully commit her features to memory. I feared that with time I'd lose even the powerful images that had imprinted already. But no-one dared take even a single photograph, fearful of preserving my heartache in the long years ahead before my daughter would *maybe* want, and maybe be deemed fit, to access her records and find me. Maybe. That's a difficult word. Five letters, but so much longing and waiting, hoping and praying packed into them. It could be a long wait until she came my way; it could be my entire lifetime, or indeed hers. Back in that hospital in 1972 the last thing everyone thought I'd need was a photograph of my baby to remind me of the child I was to lose. But as things turned out they needn't have fretted: I didn't need a picture of my child to remind me of that heart-breaking separation. The truth is, I'd never forget that agony of a mother whose child was torn away. That pain never went away. It never could. You just learn to live with it. One day at a time.

The play was written more as therapy than Great Art. A year before at the ripe old age of thirty-six I'd suffered a miscarriage – my first successful attempt at pregnancy since my only child had been taken from me all those years back. And now this second loss resonated with the first, and I found myself confronted by all the pain I'd tried so hard to lock away and keep the lid firmly on for twenty years. The hospital referred me to a counsellor this time around.

"Susan, you're a writer," she'd said softly, handing me yet another tissue as I wept away in her small sterile hospital room with its walls full of posters packed with those wise words of advice and 'relaxing' scenes.

"Why don't you just write this pain out?" she'd said. "Just pour it onto the page - let it all go for once and for all."

Of course with adoption there's no such thing as 'once and for all'. I know that now. I only suspected it then.

"Who'd want to read that?" I asked. It seemed I'd lost all belief in myself.

"It doesn't have to be for anyone else. This is for you. Just to let it all out. I'm convinced it'll help," she insisted.

"I don't know if I can," I cry. I'm crying a lot at the moment.

"Why not just have a go? Eh?"

So I do. I have a go.

After that session I walk along the river bank, unsure if I'm losing my mind. Is this what it feels like to go mad? And if it does, will this madness change all my memories of that time with my child? Just in case, before I lose it altogether, I start writing. And she's right. It does help, and I discover the therapeutic nature of putting pen to paper.

"What are you writing?" my theatre company ask when we meet.

I explain, through tears. Always tears, it seems. Endless tears for the two babies I've lost now. They want to read the play, and I promise they will when it's finished. I write deep into the night and by day I teach, watching the clock slowly tick on until I can get back to my computer and finish my story.

Within days the first draft is complete. It feels like a sack of bricks is being emptied off my back, each one examined and then neatly packed where they belong – one step removed, but still in sight if I choose to look that way. At least I feel lighter.

I take the raw, unexpurgated first draft into a stark rehearsal room, black walls and drapes with thin shafts of light illuminating the

SUSAN J BEVAN

gloom. We throw back the curtains and gather chairs in a circle. My heart is in my mouth as we read the first stage directions.

LIGHTS RISE ON A SINGLE SPOTLIGHT ON A ROCKING CHAIR, CENTRE STAGE. 'WOMAN' ROCKS GENTLY THEN STARTS TO SING A CAPELLA.

As I share for the first time what I've written, my heart pounds against my chest wall. Going back and telling the story of the hardest days and weeks of my life, my coping strategy in that rehearsal room is to stay one step removed from the real-life events. It's not easy. I bite my lip over and over as we re-member my life. At times I nearly draw blood.

So the play starts with an *a capella* song, then. A lone voice, soft and almost breaking sings it in a minor key; this voice of 'Woman' is my own as I sing:

Hush little baby, don't say a word
Mama's gonna buy you a mocking bird
And if that mocking bird don't sing
Mama's gonna buy you a diamond ring
If that diamond ring turns to brass
Mama's gonna buy you a looking glass
If that looking glass get broke
Mama's gonna buy you a billie goat
If that billie goat fall down
You'll still be the sweetest little baby in town.
So hush little baby don't say a word
Mama's gonna buy you a mocking bird
Hush little baby, don't you cry
Mama's gonna stay...right...by...your side.

The room is so still we barely breathe. Another actress takes the role over now, and in production the spotlight will fade to black and I'll leave the rocking chair centre-stage for the lights to rise on *Woman*, refilling her wine glass and taking a sip as she writes in a book. Pausing for a moment she looks up from her writing desk and speaks to her lost child, who is who-knows-where doing who-knows-what with who-knows-who.

14

THAT PICTURE OF YOU

*I wrote you a poem today. It didn't scan. And it wasn't 'Great Art'...
but it did say something about the way I feel. You can read it along with the rest,
when I meet you. 'When ....' I **will** meet you.*

Little can I imagine in my wildest dreams how prophetic that
will prove to be, and just how soon it will become reality.

So, early June 1993. Highly-charged rehearsals on *Half A
Million Women* culminate in the first of two intense dress rehearsals.
The play's title reflects the number of women who have lost their
children to adoption in the UK alone. In a couple of nights my play
will receive its world premiere, on the twenty-first anniversary of my
lost daughter's birth. Dramatic but true: a small drama studio in a side-
street in Cambridge it might be, but a world premiere it will be no less.
I'm proud of course at having written it and that this diverse group of
women think it worthy of performance, but there's no denying it's
been a long and emotional journey getting there.

Our twelve-strong all-woman theatre company has grown
unusually close over the last few months' rehearsing, working as we
are with this highly-charged material. Piecing together the scenes of
our eight days together in hospital are the hardest of all, with the
contradictions of the elation at producing such a beautiful child with
the agonising dread at losing her. But I'm not the only one to struggle.
Somehow the story and the play have resonated with each of us in
turn. Many of the company are mothers, some with children grown
up, others with teenagers, one with a young baby. Remarkably, and
unbeknown to me at the time, one of the company had herself given
birth to a baby when she was no more than a teenager. Also taken for
adoption, her child had died in the arms of his new parents shortly
before his first birthday. Was her involvement with my play maybe
cathartic for her too? I can't imagine otherwise. I just wish I'd known
at the time: maybe I could have been more of a support to her. But
she held her cards close to her chest and her story even closer to her
heart as we rehearsed day after day, week after week, material that
must at times have left her emotional scars not only raw but ripped
open, salted and left to bleed.

At the end of the long June dress rehearsal, absolutely I walk through our front door absolutely exhausted and wrung out. Heavy pregnancy and directing plays are uneasy bedfellows, I'm discovering – especially this particular play for this particular writer-director. I need a cup of chamomile tea and then to get to bed as soon as possible. I'm yawning as I shut the door behind me.

"Hi love!" I call to Bert. He's blowing his sax, and I make him jump.

"Oh! Hi!" He removes his sling from around his neck. Hiya love!"

I kiss him. We hug. I'm dead on my feet.

"How was it?"

"Yeah, great," I yawn. But before I can even get a word out about the detail of how the rehearsal went, he's ushering me towards the sofa.

"Look, I think you'd better sit down."

In that single brief moment between my husband's words and my own response, my imagination goes into overdrive, fears flying in from nowhere and everywhere like bats criss-crossing the garden just before night finally falls and the sky loses its last trace of light. And in that moment of near-panic when something unidentifiably enormous has clearly happened but I've no idea what it might be, my first thoughts go to my mother. With my father having dropped dead out of the blue like he had, was it her turn now to take a dramatic turn for the worse? Please god, not before this baby's born.

But despite being guarded Bert appears calm – half-excited even. So maybe we've received news of Arts Council funding so desperately needed if we're to develop the theatre group's work. There's even a prospect we'll become the Eastern Region's leading women's theatre company if we can only make that first step up. Funding is the key. A project grant would affirm our status as a serious contender in a game with strong odds against success for nascent players. I can see why Bert might insist I sit down.

The adrenalin rush leaves me light-headed, weakening my knees. It runs too through this baby I'll carry for another ten weeks. He shuffles and kicks as I perch on the edge of the armchair; this one prefers the calmer life, it seems.

"No, come and sit here, lovey."

Bert shifts a few books and magazines aside, clearing a space on our ample but cluttered sofa. Sitting with an arm along the back cushions, he is ready to envelop me. With his other he takes my hand tenderly, gazing fixedly on me and still smiling reassurance.

"Bert, is everything alright?" Why won't he just get on and tell me! My heart racing now, my mouth's like the Sahara. It's been too long a day and I'm beyond guessing games. I start to feel a degree of irritation.

"Yes, it's fine." He kisses me lovingly, stroking my hair. "Your sister rang."

Alarm about my mother flashes through me again, my brain racing along with my heart. Is this his way of breaking terrible news gently, thinking he's protecting me, protecting our baby?

"Why," I say, "what is it?" He squeezes my hand and smiles, his eyes filling with tears. The baby kicks a reminder that he's there too.

"Your daughter's trying to find you."

Arrival

I was born in Granny Sally's house, on my dad's side of the family, in Penywaun in the Welsh Valleys. Summer 1956. Pat Boone was Number One in the charts with 'I'll Be Home' – not that I recall it from first time round!

Originally built as a housing estate after the war, Penywaun was mainly pre-fabs at first, but now it's grown into a sprawling housing estate described as one of the most deprived in Europe. It's in an officially designated teenage pregnancy black-spot, one of a small handful in the country. In 1993 it made national news when two teenage girls frog-marched a seventy-year-old neighbour up her garden path, torturing and strangling her to death in her own shed. They used a dog chain to kill her. The whole thing particularly caught the attention of the nation because the girls went on to slash their victim's face with a Stanley knife, break eggs over her corpse, and then they tried to scalp her. She'd been stabbed more than twenty times. Under attack, the girls' families were given police protection and then re-housed when riots broke out, neighbours trying to lynch the girls' relations. That's Penywaun. That's my birthplace.

The only child of my mother's second husband, I was conceived before she was even divorced from her first. Admittedly they'd been separated for some five years by then, with Husband Number One living back up in his native Scotland. I can't imagine how it must have felt for my mother, finding herself in that situation. Bad enough to be living first with the stigma of separation in that close-knit working class community with traditional family values; but now she was a divorced mother of Anne (seven) and Peter (six), not yet married to Husband Number Two, and brazenly pregnant with me. 'Hussy!' she would have been back home. 'Slut!' The whole rigmarole must have scared her half to death. She was certainly living her life outside the norms set down in Mount at that time.

I can't even be entirely sure my parents ever did manage a wedding – certainly my brother and sister have no recollection of one, although there was something about my parents making a big trip up to nearby Aberdare to buy a ring one day when I was two or three. There's no marriage certificate to the best of my knowledge – but then, I haven't exactly gone hunting back through the registry archives. All I do know is that when I was around ten and wanting to mark their wedding anniversary just like my friend had done with her own mum and dad, she gave me very short shrift for raising the question in the first place. We were in the kitchen, with my dad shaving at the sink in his vest. I was transfixed by the way he stretched his neck, pulling his chin up with one hand while the other glided the Gillette down his stubbly throat. It fascinated me that he so rarely drew blood, and then there was the ritualistic splashing on of that aftershave that made him wince – "But you've just got to, to close the pores."

"When did you and Dad get married, Mam?"

I'm still watching the blade stroking his throat, down over his Adam's Apple. He runs the razor under the running tap, rinsing off tiny dark hairs and shaking the razor before raising it once more to his upturned chin.

"None of your business!"

"What's that?" my dad asks, nicking himself. I stare at the tiny red spot as the blood trickles down his neck.

"Nothing. Don't worry."

"I just didn't hear what..."

She speaks over him.

"Susan's asking when we got married." He stops with the razor, looking at me and then at her, not knowing what to say. It was clear who was in charge in our house.

"I told her we can't remember. Can we," my mother insists. He agrees, and that's that. He always agrees. Keeping the peace is more important than anything in our house.

I got no clearer answer weeks later in much the same situation – my father shaving over the sink, my mother feeding freshly-laundered clothes through the green, heavy mangle of the top-loading washing machine. This time I want to know why my father had hairs under his arms when my mother didn't.

"Don't be so dirty!"

I look at her, shocked. Why's that dirty!

"What kind of a question is that! Go on – get out and play!"

Lots of things went unanswered in our house – as, I suppose, in many others. Little by little you learn not to ask questions, then you learn not to say anything at all if you know what's good for you.

In any case, whatever my mother felt about being that shameful thing, 'a divorcee', she *did* finally manage to get the decree absolute from Bill before I was born, albeit with bitter resistance from Anne and Peter's father.

The journey out of that first marriage was dramatic in its own right: one bright and sunny June day in 1956, despite being achingly close to the due date for my arrival into the world, my mother and hers (Granny Ruth) with Great-Auntie Lillian in tow, took the steam train all the way up to Gretna Green in Dumfries and Galloway, just over the Scottish border. Famous for runaway brides, this was where her first marriage vows had been taken – for richer, for poorer, in sickness and in health, 'til death us do part; it hadn't lasted five years, even - and this was where she now arrived seeking a divorce, already poised to give birth to another man's child. Documents eventually signed, the three women managed by some miracle to scramble back to Mount before the labial curtain rose for my entrance onto the stage of life.

After a lengthy labour I was born on the last day of June at some unremarkable time of the day or night. My mother could never recall what time.

"How do you expect me to remember that? There's a lot of water gone under the bridge since then! You know what day it was. Isn't that enough?"

In fact I didn't know what day; I only knew the date - but that was east enough to check out. This was as close as she ever got to providing me with essential information for an astrological chart decades later. It's strange, but I'd have thought it was the kind of thing you'd remember – the time of day your child is born. I certainly recall my daughter being announced as alive, safe and well, at nine thirty am, although it was some time later when I first saw her. Our son would be born at three twenty-nine am precisely, and Bert held him straight away, still thick with mucous and streaked with blood. And me? I was truly terrified to look at him - afraid to see my new-born. Some deep resonance with that earlier birth made me petrified he too would be taken away for some reason beyond my control. But no – not this time. No-one – absolutely no-one – was taking this child from me. I'd kill before I'd lose *this* child.

"Come on," Bert said softly, cradling him in his arms. The proud dad's grin was drenched in tears. "He's beautiful - look. Come on, hold your son."

I did. And he was. Cradling him in my arms I wept with joy and love, and relief. This pink bundle was the most precious thing I'd ever set eyes on, with a crease in his forehead where he'd patiently waited in the same position for weeks until the time was right to make his calm, smooth journey into the outside world. This was the baby I would hold, the child I would raise, the man I would watch him grow into as we'd journey through life together. I held him to me, and cried – for the baby I had in my arms and for the babies I'd lost. But most of all I cried with relief and with joy and with a love like no other – the love of a mother for her child.

Three twenty-nine in the morning, a couple of hours before we'd watch the sun rise on a bright and beautiful August morning over the open Cambridge countryside, our son in our arms.

So yes, you'd think my mother might have remembered if it was daytime or night-time when I came into the world.

A long, leggy ten-pound baby, I wouldn't have been easy to birth for my diminutive mother. There would, no doubt, have been many a moment she'd rue the day they had lain together and made me. I don't think she ever truly forgave my father, several years her junior; but somehow I seemed to get away with it scot-free. I got away with everything scot-free. Nothing was ever my fault. I was to become the blue-eyed girl from the moment I drew my first breath, and we'd all of us pay some kind of price for that.

Mount

Shortly after I'm born we move to live with Granny Ruth, some five miles down the valley in Mountain Ash, 'Mount'. Population around seven thousand, Mount nestles in Mid Glamorgan some twenty miles north of Cardiff; the Cynon Valley (regularly mispronounced even by the BBC) is the least well-known of the three valleys constituting its local authority district of Rhondda-Cynon-Taf. Rhondda Fach and Rhondda Fawr lie to the West, The Taf valley, home to Merthyr Tydfil and the infamous Aberfan to the East. It was to this place at the age of eleven I'd take the long bus-trip down our valley and up the next to make cups of tea for the miners and everyone else pouring out of every hole in the black ground to dig children's bodies out of the landslide when that slag heap rumbled down the hill, engulfing an entire street and the local school in a filthy black avalanche.

It's October 21st 1966. I'm eleven years old.

"Have you heard the news?" I have, of course. Everybody has. Everything stops. It's as if they've stopped all the clocks in Christendom and beyond. The factories workers are sent home, miners are pulled back up the shafts as pit shifts abruptly ended, and someone halts the film being shown at Nixon's Hall in Mount to make an announcement in the gloom:

The tip's slid at Aberfan! It come down on the school, and there's hundreds of people need rescuing. They need every pair of hands available, so get over there right now if you can help!"

News of the disaster runs through the community fast as a landslide; before you can lift your hand to wipe the rain off your face everyone's heard. Shock reverberates through the streets, neighbours knocking on doors to tell the horrific news. Even though it's the next valley, it feels like it's our own under that suffocating sludge.

"Have you heard the news? Aberfan's slid!" No more words needed. We all know Aberfan – it's straight up and over the mountain. You'd almost have heard the screams if they hadn't been drowned out. We all know what 'sliding' they mean.

I'm First Aid trained, and so is my friend Carol, so our neighbour Auntie Flo gets us on a bus and down the valley to Ponty. Then onto another bus and up towards Merthyr. It has rained and poured for what seems like weeks, and it's *still* torrential.

We sit on the bus, wiping the condensation form the window with our sleeves to measure our progress down the narrow winding valley. The bus smells of wet wool, musty and rancid. Windscreen wipers whip across, trying to clear a view for the driver struggling to steer his way through flooding roads and rivulets. Despite the sand bags laid to hold back the flooding river, the whole valley is awash, black as ink and like a watercolour as we wind our way down past Abercynon. It's a scene from Blake, a vision of despair; no-one could have imagined anything darker than this. But then no-one could have imagined what we were to find in Aberfan.

The glaring contrast in the small town tonight is unimaginable. Black as night, black as pitch, the landslide has spewed slurry like a river, running in a tidal wave down the mountain, over the railway embankment, over the village, over Pantglas Junior School and over twenty nearby houses. Bleak like you can't imagine, and the souls of everyone there black as death. It's a blackness for many that will never again let any life into their lives. The water-logged tip had finally collapsed - after repeated warnings to the National Coal Board - like a sandcastle dropping away as the sea pulls back, taking with it cranes and trucks, trams and trees, corrugated roofs and telegraph poles. And lives - so many young lives. No parent should have to suffer this, but so many do on this fateful night.

By the time we arrive the lights of the emergency services, harsh and blinding, cast a dazzling glare on the scene of carnage before us. It's a vision truly from hell that no-one can ever capture. Imaginations don't stretch to this.

Torrents of rain still teem from the sky and the fear is there might yet be another slide. Everyone does their best, but their best can never be enough with all those children dying in that filthy slurry, drowned and suffocated by the hellish muck that engulfed their school. Women and men alike weep as the rescue mission gets under way, struggling to shift another and another and yet one more bucketful of the black filth under which so many little bodies are buried.

First Aiders or not though, there's not much we at the age of eleven can actually do to help. We make tea, put the occasional plaster on people; we carry things from here to there, but to tell the truth we feel helpless and pathetic. Certainly the last thing the men need – and it's mostly men (the miners coming off their shifts with their helmet lights still on, are magnificent) – the last thing those brave men need is us youngsters under their feet. Nonetheless even our lame presence is welcomed with warmth, as long as we don't impede the gruelling work of shifting tons and tons of suffocating muck. We've turned out to support, and that's what counts as far as the desperate town in concerned. We're offering any support we can, and the small contribution we *can* make has made that long journey down one grim valley and up the next on this unforgettable night worth every shivering, miserable moment.

One hundred and forty-four people are killed at Aberfan on October 21st, 1966. One hundred and forty-four. A hundred and sixteen of them are children. The tip slid at 9.15 am; no-one was rescued alive after eleven that morning. It was a whole week before they recovered the last of the bodies. The torment of that loss was and remains beyond what any parent should have to suffer. My mother worked with a woman whose daughter had woken up that morning not wanting to go to school. Truancy wasn't part of valley life back then; you went to school unless you were dying. We all went with coughs and colds all winter. So there'd been a row in that house. Mam was determined her daughter was going to school. Daughter cried. Mam packed her off. Daughter kicked up a stink. But she set off for school. She walked halfway up the road then turned around and slunk home, crying that she felt too ill to go.

"What's wrong with you, then?"

"I don't know!"

"So get to school. Now!"

"No! I don't want to!" she whined.

With no time left to argue before setting off for work, the mother left her daughter with Granny. That little girl's life was saved by not being at Pantglas Junior that fateful day. When the announcement was made at the factory that the tip had slid at Aberfan and the school had been in its path, my mother saw first-hand just how precious a child's life could be.

That was Aberfan. 1967. Let it never be forgotten. Like the Bangladeshi factory that collapsed with a death toll of more than a thousand as I write this, there had been warnings of impending disaster. Life is cheap in late capitalism. We know this far too well all over the world in mining communities. It should not be.

Mount sprawls along the River Cynon, black with coal in the seventies before the pits were closed in that disgraceful, barbaric attack on mining communities by the government of the day. The town winds its way along the shallow mineral-rich trench of land alongside the railway, closed for decades but now re-opened down to Abercynon, Pontypridd and, at the end of the line Cardiff, the capital of Wales. A Celtic cross found up above Mount suggests Christian worship or burial here dates back as far as the ninth century.

Not quite a town and functioning like - though rather bigger than - a village, Mount is full of contradictions. Easily caricatured as inbred, inward-looking and insular, many of us did seem relatively untouched by its natural beauty, taking it casually for granted. It's easy to get used to something when you're born into it. Or at least appear to.

"If only..." a retired headmistress friend said to me once, "If only they'd raise their sights."

"Do you mean literally or metaphorically?" asks my sixteen-year-old self, probably feeling I have to impress my boyfriend's mother – and I am, after all, studying A Level English, her specialism. I feel the urge to prove I'm worthy of her only son.

"Both," she replies. "I mean, look at these hills. How can you live under those and not find your spirits raised when you lift your eyes? And if you raise a man's spirit - or a woman's, Susan - you can raise their sights. Just lift up your head. You don't have to look down at the ground under your feet the whole time. There's a whole world out there. It takes just a little imagination, sheer determination and hard work, and you can be a part of a bigger picture."

The same woman introduced me at the age of sixteen to *Winnie The Pooh* when my English teacher invited me to read to the junior reading club he'd set up. Despite initial scepticism on my part, the book was an inspiration. It was the one I would buy for our son's first birthday twenty years later.

Yes, we *were* focused at the ground beneath our feet, because that's where so many got their living back then. There have, of course, always been enormous economic and political forces at work and maybe now more than ever in recent history we're all too aware of how disempowered the so-called common man is in this complexly interwoven globalised world. But the natural environment surrounding Mount – those verdant hills, ferrous brooks and lush hilltop pastures, rich in fern and bracken – these are gifts I've left behind with a great deal of *hiraeth*, living as I do now in flat, intensively-farmed East Anglia. I miss the huge smooth slabs of rock in the middle of the narrow river weaving its way through the Cwm up over the mountain, where we jumped into rock pools on hot summer days away from parents' prying eyes. (Yes, every summer was hot and every rock pool fresh, as memories reconstruct them with time.) I miss the Gorsedd stone circle tucked quietly away in the blue-belled carpets of Duffryn Woods, on my daily walk to school. And I miss the sense of community. Rose-coloured my spectacles may be, but the coal-mining valleys in their day truly were full of contradictions like these.

Our secondary school was one such contradiction. It was, I see now with the clarity that only comes with distance, an enormous privilege to be educated in Dyffryn House, the Gothic mansion that had been Lord Aberdare's former home. The grounds alone were breath-taking – more characteristic of a grand Victorian estate than a comprehensive school of a thousand mostly working-class pupils - with the biggest holly bush in Wales dominating the grassed area in front of the house, and a shallow stream meandering through the wooded grove at the far end of the playing fields. The collection of ornamental trees gracing the grounds spoke to us of the world beyond Mount if only we'd listen, beyond Wales, beyond Europe even – a world full of mystery and wonder for a thirteen-year-old arriving in this picture-book estate, wide-eyed and enquiring if only we took the time to raise our sights and look around us.

The school's oak-panelled library with gargantuan fireplace, high ornate ceilings and thick wooden balustrades curving down the broad central staircase were absolutely unlike anything we Valleys kids would have seen first-hand in our entire lives. The Welsh have always known the value of education – it was one of the few ways to escape the limited life chances afforded by the valleys even in their heyday.

And despite – or maybe because of - the poverty pervading Mount, it produced some extraordinary local heroes. Elaine Morgan, for instance, still lives in her terraced house in the Caegarw area. Born in 1920 into a poor local family, she won a scholarship to read English at Oxford. Arriving and asking for directions to Lady Margaret Hall, her thick Welsh accent led to the assumption she was there to take up a cleaning job. No stereotyping there, then, Elaine. This woman went on to become a ground-breaking anthropologist, internationally feted and shifting the course of an increasingly phallocentric evolutionary theory to a scientific field in which both sexes played their roles in human development. Contributor to the marvellous TED Talks at the age of *eighty-eight* and award-winning writer, Elaine's TV dramatisation of Vera Brittain's *A Testament of Youth* was generally regarded as her greatest accomplishment; but her most populist contribution to the world of The Arts was her scribing of countless episodes of Dr Finlay's Casebook and Z Cars! Asked where she found so many great original storylines, she reputedly replied, "Well, you just go and queue in the shops in Mount and you hear it all." She's said to have hurried home from shopping trips, eager to get it all down while it was still fresh in her mind.

I wonder, just how versatile and talented does a woman have to be before she becomes a household name? This truly Renaissance woman is still writing today, having published in 2005 the incisive *Pinker's List: The New Darwinists and The Left.* (You can work out her age at the time.) When I took *Half A Million Women,* my own play about my daughter's adoption, back to Wales I was enormously privileged to be invited to tea with Elaine Morgan. I sat slack-jawed at the feet of this little, shy, modest, artistic and intellectual giant. So Elaine is still proving my ex-headmistress friend right: here is a woman whose sights certainly aren't solely on the ground beneath her feet.

We had our share of notable men too, to be fair. Born and raised in Mount, Howard Collins was a school-friend of my brother. At the age of seven Pete found himself out one day exploring the fields across the valley with the fearless Collins. They were the wrong side of the river as night started to fall, with no quick way back. It would be a good twenty minutes to get home via the playing fields and the main road. But luckily there was a black metal pipe some ten inches in diameter crossing the River Cynon: not wide, but *just* wide enough to walk across if your balance was absolutely perfect and your nerve rock steady, with the light of day on your side. Anxious seven-year-olds, and with dusking rapidly turning to dark, nothing was in their favour. It would be an act of sheer recklessness to try to take a short-cut across this treacherous route.

"Come on, Pete!" called Collins. "There's a short-cut here!"

And before Peter even had to time to register exactly what his friend was proposing, the fearless Collins was off in the fast-fading light at breakneck speed.

"Hang on!" Peter calls after him. "Watch out!"

"Nah, it's fine. Come on, Pete!" And then silence.

Nerves of steel and the step of an angel, that boy had. Now even at that tender age Peter was astonished at this boy's determination and focus. Like a top-class gymnast Collins placed one careful step in front of the other, his arms spread out to help him balance, and his head as still as the tiger creeps up on its prey. Another step, and he was mid-river, the deep water flowing fast and furious, coal-dust black as the rivers of hell, some fifteen feet below him. Holding his breath, Pete was terrified his friend would fail to make it across. In equal measure he was terrified he *would*, giving Pete little option but to follow. Holding his breath with his fear rising like bile from his very core, Peter watched as Collins took his final step, arriving at the other end with speed and grace. He turned, grinning.

"Come on Pete!"

My brother took his first step onto the pipeline, listening to the rush of the water some twenty feet below. His heart was banging like a djembe drum. He did not dare look at the river, rapidly flowing coal-black down the valley and out of sight. Like most children of his age in Mount, Peter had never learned to swim. Nor probably had Howard Collins.

"It's fine Pete. Just don't look down. Keep looking at me."

Arms out. Just like Howard. One foot then the next, his eyes fixed on the smut-caked pipe ahead of him. Just like Howard, Peter carefully picked his way across, steady as he could manage with panic rising in waves.

"That's great Pete – just keep looking at me. Go on. You're doing great!"

The whole way across Collins talked Pete through. Fearless in his focus, controlled and coordinated as a champion racehorse, Howard was able even as a young boy to channel his energy to any challenge. A phenomenal individual, and a quite remarkable friend, he left Pete decades later with a deep sense of privilege at having shared some of his formative years with this boy from up the street in Miskin.

And the best known of all in the valley is a name familiar to everyone born and raised in Mount: Guto Nyth Bran. A local sports legend, a statue of him in the town centre commemorating his athletic prowess. But he is particularly remembered every New Year's Eve when the Nos Galan (literal translation *Night Race*) is run through the streets of Mountain Ash. Now an afternoon race and a shadow of its former self, it was in its heyday an event attracting hundreds of runners from all over the world, starting with a late-night church service in nearby Llanwonno, a tiny hamlet high up on the mountainside. From here a torch was carried Olympic-style by a mystery runner who wound his or her way down the dark mountain road, through forest and woodland to finally start the race at Mount Town Hall. Thousands of people turned out from pubs, clubs and parties, and some just stood on their own front step, waiting for the runners to pass by, locals running side by side with international athletes. It wa a great democratiser, the Nos Galan. A great buzz of excitement filled the air as speculation grew about who the mystery runner might be this year, the event having been graced in the past by such luminaries as Olympic gold medallists Mary Rand and Nicole Cook, and Welsh international rugby stars Stephen Jones and Shane Williams.

Guto himself was born in Llwyncelyn in the Rhondda, but he ran his first competitive race over the Nos Galan route. Growing up tending sheep for his father, legend has it that his running prowess was first identified when he caught a hare in flight. He's said to have been able to run to Ponty and back before his mother's kettle boiled. Given the distance of some seven miles, either he was runner of some stature or the kettle was remarkably inefficient - or enormous. Either way a local shopkeeper and subsequent sponsor, Siân O'Shop, arranged for him to run against an unbeaten English captain over a distance of four miles across Hirwaun Common. Guto took the race with consummate ease, winning four hundred pounds and a reputation which drew opponents from far and wide. Such was his talent, however, that competition soon dwindled with fewer and fewer bothering to challenge; gradually he stopped running altogether.

At the age of thirty-seven, though, Guto was persuaded out of retirement to run a gruelling head-to-head race against a new star known as 'Prince'. The prize money stood at a thousand guineas – a fortune to Guto Nyth Bran as to most of Mount in those days. Training began in earnest and he was soon back to form.

Prince took an early lead in the gruelling twelve-mile race, but in a dramatic finish Guto found a store of energy which sent him charging up the final hill and winning in an astonishing fifty-three minutes. As he gasped for breath, his sponsor Siân O'Shop ran over and gave him a hefty congratulatory slap on the back. It was to prove a fatal blow. Struggling for his last breath as his heart jumped out of place, Guto Nyth Bran dropped down dead on the spot. Grief-stricken his supporters carried his lifeless body over to Llanwonno grave, where his bones lie buried.

So Mount has its share of notables, some internationally famous and still much-celebrated, others less widely so. But Mount wasn't a place to remain invisible whoever you were; not a place to keep yourself to yourself, try as you might. In my day Mount's local school, 'the comp' as it was known, boasted war poet Alun Lewis's widow as one of its modern language teachers. His beautiful poetry lives on in his *Collected* Poems. Everyone in Mount would know that our wonderful poet Lewis had married Gweno in 1941 as a Royal Engineer. He sailed for India in 1942, and was then despatched to Burma in 1944. Everyone in Mount would know that he'd been found dead in Burma, shot in what the army declared an accident with his own pistol, and that it had been found in his own hand. Everyone in Mount would know that Gweno never went on to re-marry, at least to the best of my knowledge, and every pupil would learn quickly that she taught the German language with a rod of iron, dressed always in what looked like mourning. Now I understand, of course. But back then in Mount, although everybody would have known, none would have spoken. Not openly. I was to find out first-hand how it felt to have everybody know, and none to speak.

Granny

Forty-seven Clarence Street was a small, rented, terraced house with two bedrooms – one for my parents, one for me and Granny, and a box room for Anne and Peter. It sat behind the tiniest of front gardens, hemmed in by a neat box hedge which is there to this very day. The smell of the privet, so sweet it must surely be cultivated for that alone, evokes that house like nothing else - other than *Lily of The Valley*, Granny's favourite perfume and her parma violet sweets.

At one end of the house just inside the front door, the electric meter sat high out of my reach; at the other end fourteen steep stone steps led down to the garden and the coal cwtch, dark as the pitch from the coal itself. Every winter Granny had a delivery of a 'hool ton of coal', free from the Coal Board – Gransha had been a miner, ending his working life driving steam locomotives for the NCB, happy as a sandboy by all accounts. He died of a heart attack, like so many of the men back then, before I was born and not long after Peter's birth. My mother would tell me of how his eyes lit up when she'd take baby Anne in her pram down to see belovéd Gransha at dinner time, thick white bricks of sandwiches carefully wrapped in the greaseproof wrapper the bread had arrived in, a flask of tea tucked into the bottom of the pram.

On delivery day the coal truck pulled up outside house after house, depositing its black treasure in mounds from the bottom of the street to the top. Most families were tied in to the mines in one way or another. The driver black from flat cap to solid heavy boots, thick gloves on powerful hands manoeuvring the truck into place as he would hang from the door, twisted and stretched to judge the truck's position within an inch. No power steering back then, and the muscles standing proud on those forearms told it all. The whole way up the street stood those tidy pyramids of coal, some pieces large as boulders, half-filling a bucket in one fell swoop: they'd have to be sledge-hammered down in the coal cwtch later. Others made up the 'small coal', useful for keeping the fire ticking over; and finally there was a load that was practically pure dust. This would be shovelled straight onto a roaring fire, damping it down to slow the burning, extending the fire's life.

Granny understood the exact role played by every shape and size of coal, a melange of fuel awaiting the magical mixing of the pyrotechnic genius – our Gran.

The driver pushing a switch in his cab, we children watched transfixed as he raised the truck hydraulically – by wizardry to our young eyes. Up and up it went until it looked like it could rise no further without spewing its load over the top. Then it came to a halt and, climbing down from his seat, the driver walked around to the back for the umpteenth time that day, lifting the latch and spilling the contents on the edge of the pavement in our own little mountain of glistening Welsh riches. A cloud of dust rising to envelop him, it gets us too if we're not far enough back, the oily smell catching the back of your throat as you breathe, minute particles shimmering like tiny black jewels in the sunlight.

Then the work would start, the whole ton having to be carried bucket by bucket by bucket down the fourteen steep stone steps to the garden, to the coal cwtch as big as a good-sized room. At four, five years old I'm allowed to join in, a near-empty bucket dangling between my skinny legs. One piece, two pieces….

"No, that one's too big, Susan. Leave that for Peter."

Granny knew he'd move heaven and earth for her – even the 'hool' ton if she so much as glanced in his direction.

Struggling a couple of steps at a time with my battered galvanised metal bucket before dropping it for a breather, I was determined to pull my weight. To help us along we sang.

"There's a hole in my bucket, dear Liza, dear Liza..."

There was an absolute *pile* of coal to shift. And if Granny could do it with her bad bones, there's no way I was wimping out! All the way down those fourteen steps with their view right across the valley, gripping the wobbly wooden handrail while the bucket tried its damnedest to swing me off balance, I'd take one step at a time, climb up into the coal cwtch and tip my paltry few pieces onto the mound as high as my head, then head straight back up for another bucket. Another three lumps, another descent. There always seemed to be more steps to be taken in Granny's. Up, down; up… And all the coal had to be tipped onto the right pile in the cwtch – big coal all off to the left and towards the back, securely stacked in its pen, then the small coal along the right-hand wall, and finally the dustiest of all over in the nearest right-hand corner, just inside the door.

Newspaper laid all the way through the house, we'd try our best to stop the coal being walked everywhere, stop it seeping into every nook and cranny. Then finally, with the whole lot down in the cwtch, it was time to wash the pavement down with buckets of clean fresh water. Newspaper lifted ready for starting the next day's fire, we'd all gather at the huge bosh just inside the back door, scrubbing hands and arms under the freezing cold tap, the only running water in the house - the same back door I'd cry into with earache, banging my head against the wooden panels trying to get some relief, the draught shooting up my trouser legs and making me shiver as I sobbed. Snot and tears mingled as they run down my face and were wiped away into my sleeve.

At the bottom of the same fourteen steep stone steps was the only toilet for the six of us. I sit there in the dark of night with Granny – three, four, five years old – on the long, wooden slat of a toilet. She sits beside me, her body warm next to mine in the freezing cold, pitch black, the candle casting shadows on the grey stone walls.

"You finished yet, gul?"

I'm three, and she's been telling me stories by the light of a flickering candle, my feet dangling above the grey stone floor and my knickers around my knees.

"No, not yet." I'm shivering with cold, wrapped in a coarse army surplus blanket. It smells of moth balls. And of course I've finished, but another story makes the bitter cold worthwhile. "I'll try again!" And while I 'try again' she sings to me.

Pack up your troubles in your old kit bag
And smile…

I learn all the old war songs in that toilet. It's our special place. Owls serenade us, wooing through the small hours before dawn. And as the light begins to rise over The Tumpy across the valley in those early morning visits, Mr Beynon's cock crows to wake the dead - not that they ever sleep. Not in Granny's house.

The dead keep their eyes closely fixed on all of us, all the time. Ghosts everywhere. Coming back from the séance with Granny, the dead stand over the cradle when baby Anne stands at the doors of death, rheumatic fever raging through her infant body. She remembers seeing a bright light one night as she lay in her cot, and an angel's face appearing. The angel says nothing, but Anne knows she's there to look after her. There had been times when Anne hadn't been expected to pull through. Her angel was having none of that.

Behind Granny's chair, beside the hearth, at the bottom of the bed….the dead people made themselves very much at home in Granny's house. Who wouldn't, I ask now.

I sleep with Granny until I'm five, and she goes to bed when I go to bed. No luxury of a light-switch upstairs and down, so we climb the stairs in moving shadows. She looks massive in silhouette on the wall in her long white nightie, solid earthenware water bottle in one hand, dulled brass candlestick dripping with wax in the other.

We climb into the enormous bed we share, and make animal shadows on the walls…a rabbit, a crocodile. The frost on the inside of the window makes icy human figures. Maybe they're ghosts, too. The wind, whistling round the rattling window-pane, kisses the candle flame, scattering shadows around the dimly lit room. And she reads to me. She reads and reads. A huge, heavy hardback book of fairy tales, colour pictures catching my child's eye in the warm, dancing circle of light spilling onto the book and beyond. I can barely lift the tome, but she opens the shiny slippery cover and spreads it across our knees. We begin at the very beginning.

"Once upon a time…"

Cinderella, Snow White, Little Red Riding Hood - her finger follows the words on the page, my eyes following her finger. Her body sinks into the heavy bolster and feather pillow and I sink into her slight body, melting into the fairy-tale.

I can read long before I go to nursery and one day as Granny stands at the gate-post ready to pass the time of day with anyone and everyone, my headmistress stops to speak to her.

Never seen outside school without a hat, Miss Price carries a series of children's notebooks tucked underneath her slender arm. Beneath them, draped firmly at her elbow is a black leather handbag big enough to hold several more. "Like a pin in paper," Granny describes her, dressed as she is in an outfit lending as much to 'make do and mend' as it does to Christian Dior. Her suit with its full skirt, soft shoulders and tight waist serves to emphasise her hour-glass figure, and yet her demeanour suggests she is unaware of the effect she has on the male of the species. Local men visibly cower before the headmistress, confronted as they are by this 1950s chic; she herself has never worked out why they avert their eyes in passing. The combination of eau de puissance and their own school-hood memories of freezing urinals, repeated failure, and canings from school authorities, mingle inevitably to make Miss Price a particularly contradictory specimen of womanhood.

"Hallo Mrs. Smith."

"Hallo Miss Price," Granny smiles.

"Your Susan is a very good reader, Mrs Smith."

"Is she really, Miss Price?"

"She really is. Very good *indeed*, Mrs Smith."

"Oh! Well, thank you very much Miss Price. Thank you very much."

Sounding astonished and delighted though Granny does, she knows full well of course. I've learned to read and much, much more snuggled up cosy and warm in bed with her. I learned that Granny stood for no nonsense, for one thing. Once cold, that stone water bottle was out of that bed, flying to the ground with a thud to wake the dead - if indeed they ever slept at all in our house! Any poor sod sat downstairs would leap out of their skin as that bottle smacked into the floor: that bed was some three feet off the ground and the bottle weighed a ton. But no; it was cold, and it had no place being pussy-footed around with – not in Granny's bed, it didn't. Thud! It's where we said our prayers every night, too. She'd been raised a Baptist, with her father a lay preacher with real 'hwyl' it was said. But pray though I might, until the moment of her death God never granted me the joy of seeing Granny relieved from the crippling pain in those poor buckled legs and that chronically bowed spine, of the relentless march of her dreadful Paget's disease.

SUSAN J BEVAN

School

I did well in school – always – and I was happy there. It was a place to play, safe, and to do fun things. Some of them even had an academic purpose. As I say, I was reading well before I started nursery, Granny making sure of that in her own quiet, loving way. And I can't say I found any real challenge with anything academic throughout my school career. Except maybe the Van de Graaff Generator – I never got even close to getting that! Chemistry too. How does *anyone* get Chemistry!

My Infants school was at the top of our street, just across from St John's Church where I would later get myself confirmed when I needed support from somewhere – *anywhere* – after losing my daughter. It was God I turned to in my search for someone to hold and to care for me – to love me. Totally selfish it was, my motivation. Any port in an emotional storm.

A foreboding building to a four-year-old, Clarence Street Infants stood in grey Welsh stone aloft a grassy bank running up from the top of what felt at the time to be a very tall wall. It was certainly much taller than the infant me. We weren't allowed to walk around this front side of the school for fear of an accident or high-jinx. Black iron railings stood proud of the wall, preventing illicitly roaming children from rolling down the bank and tumbling with a crash over the edge and down six or seven feet onto the pavement. These days a Risk Assessment box could confidently be signed that all consideration had been given to child welfare – except, of course, the remaining risk of rolling down the bank straight into the unforgiving angular railings themselves. Looking up from the road, four steeply-pitched roofs rose high above second-floor windows. Behind the glass stood an enormous assembly hall where camp beds would be laid out for a mid-afternoon rest, infant eyes compelled to close perchance to sleep under coarse green army surplus blankets - the only cover from the valley's winter's chill.

Most of what I remember about Infants school involves food or fun. I guess that's how infant school should be. First thing after Assembly we'd line up at Miss's desk, dinner money clutched tight in tiny fists, coins burning holes in our flesh from fear of dropping them. I carried mine to school in my glove, tucked tight in my hand for safe-keeping. Granny's idea, that was. And then at break-time, the quarter-bottle of full-fat milk, frozen in harsh winter when the frost still lies thick on the ground, silver tops pecked open before we'd a chance to get our hands on them; a rich tea biscuit, one for each child, from the shiny crinkly deep blue packet - fat little fingers fumbling to break the seal.

I was Biscuit Monitor and had to fight the urge to give double helpings to skinny waif Tommy whose jumpers unravelled at the sleeve, and who always smelled of stale pee and poo. Nobody wanted to sit next to Tommy because he stank, and you could see the nits walking on his hair. We all knew they jumped miles in nit distance. Miss made sure he sat in the end row, where desks were singles to fit us all in the room. That way nobody had to sit next to Tommy. It was a sensible measure. We still got nits.

Bladders regularly neared bursting, and actually did on one occasion for one of my poor friends, in the agonising struggle to avoid school toilets. Reeking of urine they were, wind whipping up bare legs, your best friend holding the door closed in the absence of locks, and boys bursting in when your knickers were down.

Dinner time was all about communal games after steaming treacle sponge and hot lumpy custard – OK if you thought that was how school food was meant to be, and we knew no different of course.

What's the time, Mr Wolf? One o'clock! What's the time Mr Wolf? Every rain-free dinner time, creeping up on whoever was the far end of the playground, bursting with excitement if you were nearly the last one in. *The farmer's in his den, the farmer's in his den, ee-i-adio….* desperate to be the farmer's wife - or not, depending on who the farmer was. *Absolutely* desperate not to be the dog and get a pounding on your back from every other child giving you a 'pat' (aka beating). Then home to Granny, just down the road in number forty-seven, past the house where her sister would later take her own life sitting in bed in her downstairs bedroom, the back parlour of her daughter's family home. She'd had enough of being 'a burden' on them, herself in advanced stages of Paget's Disease too, and practically bed-bound. She'd tied a plastic bag over her head with Christmas ribbon one December and suffocated herself, her young grandson being sent running down the street to tell Granny she had to 'Come quick!' but with no hint of what to lay ahead of her. Granny had done her best to hobble past the dozen houses in double-quick time, sensing something terrible had to be up. It would have exhausted her just getting there, but the shock of walking into that bedroom and seeing her own sister, dead eyes staring at her through the clear plastic, Christmas ribbon neatly tied around her neck and dead eyes staring out. It must have come close to killing my gran on the spot.

So I walk down past Auntie Sis's house on my way home from school, then past my friend Janice's with her crazy black Labrador, 'Nigger' as he was extraordinarily called. Even more extraordinarily no-one ever questioned it. I guess we didn't in the sixties. Finally I'd pass Mr Knight's.

"Don't ever go in Mr Knight's, even if he asks you. Not even if he offers you sweets. Do you understand, Susan?"

"Yes." I'm five. Granny's insistent.

Inevitably he asks. Predictably I go. Five is a very trusting age. Sitting on his knee doesn't seem so bad. Mrs Knight is never anywhere to be seen. He gives me sweets. They're nice. I like jelly babies and take time deciding which bits to bite off first. Once I know that's all that happens, I don't go again - no matter how many sweets he offers me, and much as I like jelly babies. Granny said not to.

We were an odd lot in Clarence Street.

Old Friends

Forty-seven Clarence Street had been Granny's home all her life, and she'd made it a very safe haven for us children. Being virtually housebound, her world had progressively closed down around her, until she finally couldn't leave the house with any ease as her disease progressed. The furthest Granny had managed to walk in my young days was Mrs Cookaine's a few doors down for a natter at the gatepost. But even this took an act of will and a gathering of strength as she struggled along past three or four tiny front gardens, holding onto the low walls to support her as her curved bones strained under the pressure of carrying even this tiny frame of hers. By the time I was to hit my teens this short sojourn would become too much for her, and she would effectively be imprisoned in her own home.

Legs bowed to rival John Wayne after a month in the saddle, and stooped with that severe curvature of her spine, Ruth Smith the senior (my mother too was Ruth) stood no more than five foot tall. Raising her sights from the ground must have been agony, but she did it nonetheless. 'Downcast' was something she'd never have understood, and you'd be hard-pressed to find someone with more humour in her heart and generosity in her soul than Ruth the elder. She loved a laugh, and relished the stories of valleys nonsense people regaled to her as they passed and stopped.

In earlier photographs Granny stands proud in every sense above my mother and her niece Auntie Lillian, shoulder-length dark hair falling in cherubic ringlets about her face. A slim, cheerful woman with a direct gaze for the camera, small-waisted and fine-boned, it's not hard to imagine why Gransha'd fallen in love with her. Nor was he the first. Her first husband had been killed mysteriously in London: something to do with an exploding zeppelin, but we could never quite get the details out of her. "Oh, you don't want to know too much about him!"

Granny exuded love for everyone, it seemed. It seeped out of her pores as if she had found the land of milk and honey and spent half a lifetime bathed in it, soaking it up ready to dole back out – but especially for us three grandchildren who'd had the privilege to grow up with her.

Immobile though she was, Granny tried her best to make the most of life and she never lost her sense of fun. Sit for hours on end she would, with Mrs Kinnearly, chewing the fat. Gran's blind Irish friend lived just down the road with her dog, Blackie. When I was four, the diminutive Mrs Kinnearly scared the living daylights out of me. White as white, she was: thin fine white hair stuck flat on her scalp, dead white eyes behind dark glasses, paper-thin white skin, and white whiskers on her chin. She walked with a white stick, with her white-whiskered, jet black Labrador dog at her heels. He must have been getting on, too.

"Your Tom's behind you there, Ruth," she suddenly announces out of nowhere. My Gransha had died years before I was born.

"He's saying you shouldn't be worrying about your Idris."

"How can I not, tell him." Granny stokes the fire.

"He's going to be alright, Ruth. He says, don't you worry. He's looking out for him."

Reading Granny's tea leaves one day Mrs Kinnearly tells her, "Somebody's going to crack their head open, Ruth. You mark my words. There'll be crying before the day's out. You watch if there isn't."

And there was, within the hour.

There were metal railings at the bottom of Clarence Street where it turned into Bailey Street - one of the steepest roads in Mount. They were designed to stop you slipping down the slope going from the pavement to the grey stone garden walls running twenty feet below. But to me they were parallel bars, and I was an Olympic gymnast – even though I'd never heard of the Olympics back then. I could spend hours on end swinging upside down, looping the loop. Knickers or no knickers on show, it was great fun and cost nothing. I was pretty adept even if I say so myself. But playing that day with Janice, adeptness was in short supply; ambition gone to my head I'd lost my grip as I spun upside down, cracking down and banging my head on the pavement. Hitting the concrete I gave a blood-curdling, blood-pouring howl. I started to run straight up the street to Granny's. I screamed the place down with Janice in tow, my friend trying her best to work the magic of a five-year-old nurse.

"Rub it."

"Whah!"

"Let me kiss it better."

"Whaah!"

"It works when Mam does it!"

"Whaaah! Graaannyyy!"

Sometimes Mrs Kinnearly came out with big pronouncements of global significance: "Hailio Salasio says there's going to be trouble with the Arabs, Ruth. You mark my words. Never wrong, he's not. Oh no. Not Hailio Salasio. There'll be trouble with them Arabs. You watch if there's not."

And there was.

'Hailio Salasio' (sic) was Mrs Kinnearly's spirit guide and he followed her everywhere. He scared me stiff too, even though I'd never actually seen him. Granny described him as a tall, refined black man, in a long white robe and something like a towel wrapped round his head. He'd been a doctor when he was alive, and he was softly spoken. Very gentle man. He hadn't actually spoken to her, but Mrs Kinnearly told her all about him, right down to the finest detail. He was gentle through and through, she said, and full of wisdom.

There were a lot of dead people in Granny's house. She was really happy about it. She liked company.

The two women sit for hours in the ancient matching winged armchairs either side the open fire, watching for faces in the burning embers. I think there must be ghosts in there, too. They wait for the soot-clad kettle to boil on the stove - built into either side of the hearth, it is. It sits all day on the range, but gets shifted over to the fire proper when a cup of PG Tips is on the agenda – which is pretty regularly. Granny liked her PG Tips. She didn't buy 'rubbish'. Always quality for Granny, from Mr Freeman in the corner shop where the gully runs down to Albert Street, Consort Street and the regally named but rather more earthy Victoria Street.

Granny'd been a loyal customer at Mr Freeman's food and general grocery emporium for years, first in person with a chat and a laugh – the large rugged man always had a joke or a story waiting for her, much of it involving characters in Mount - then later through us little messengers. Whenever she sent me down to buy something for her – ham, cheese, Camp coffee – he'd say, "Is that for Mrs Smith?" and then give me the best. I'd watch him in his faded brown overall taking slices of a huge ham as if he were producing a piece of lace for the Queen of England, his razor-sharp knife teasing off the paper-thin slices. You could almost see through them.

"She likes it nice and thin, does Mrs Smith. Tell her I done it special for her. Here, have a toffee."

Everybody respected Mrs Smith, despite the goings-on of her only daughter. Everybody knew about the shenanigans, of course. Everybody knew, but nobody spoke about it. Not openly. And poor Granny just carried on as if nothing untoward was going on.

*　　*　　*　　*

Reading to me one night in that enormous bed with its heavy silk quilt and plump goose-feather bolster, Granny suddenly stopped in her tracks.

"Oh!"

"What?"

"It's alright, bach. Don't worry. It's only Hailio Salasio."

It's not what I expect in the middle of Jack and The Bean Stalk. Jack was racing to get back to the top of the stalk and escape before the giant caught up with him, and that was scary enough in itself without Hailio Salasio turning up in our bedroom willy nilly. He should be in Mrs Kinnearly's house, where he belonged.

"Don't worry."

But I do worry. I slide down the bolster, further under the blankets and closer to Granny.

"Where is he?"

"Who? Jack?"

"No – the ghost."

"Oh. At the bottom of the bed. Take no notice. It's alright – he's only come to listen to the story. Just let him be."

So I let him be – even though I don't know exactly where he is. It's not easy ignoring people when you don't know exactly where they are. I curl up closer again, and Granny cwtches me close by, reading softly. And before I know it I'm asleep, dreaming the dreams of a five-year-old who lives with the dead people. And sometimes, before dawn, when the miners make their way back from the night shift, singing as they walk up the street, skin as black as pitch in the coal black dark of the night, with the rest of Mount fast asleep, their voices drift into my dreams. But I'm alright. I'm curled up safe and tight in Granny's arms. We all need dreams. And arms to hold us.

SUSAN J BEVAN

The Dark House

I'm five when we move out of Granny's and into The Dark House. The Dark House has brown walls, brown floors and brown doors, and there's nothing I like about it. It's ten minutes' walk from Granny's – up towards the top of Clarence Street where St John's Church was, down the steep slopes of Mount Pleasant Terrace, impassable when iced over with frozen snow as it was in 1963 for weeks on end, when we kids made it no better sledging down on tin trays, Then it's along past the back of Auntie Flo's house, next door to Carol Stone's. Carol is my best friend.

So The Dark House in Hughes Street isn't so very far away from Granny's, but for us three children we might as well have been those pioneering migrants who left for Patagonia a century and a half before. Just like them, we too were leaving behind everything we'd ever been able to call 'home'.

Granny's house is a complete contrast to The Dark House in the same way a lover's fingers caress but the hands of an assailant abuse from that first beguiling touch. Granny's house is rented, where The Dark House comes with a mortgage which means my dad literally working himself into an early grave. Granny's house full of the dead people, The Dark House is lifeless, no soul to be found there. Hers is unaltered in all thirty-seven years she's lived there, first with Gransha, then with all of us and now finally on her own. The Dark House will eventually have every mod con - a bathroom, a shower, central heating, an indoor toilet. But never a phone, and that was to be a key factor in another chapter in our lives.

"It's alright," my mother says about leaving Granny's fire behind. "We'll have a Rayburn put in. It's like a fire, but different."

44

And as for leaving Granny's garden, the steps and the coal cwtch, my brother's old rusted toy car down in the long grass?

"I'll put a swing in the garden for you," my dad adds.

But none of that makes a scrap of difference because the bottom line is there's no Granny. And come to that, it's not just Granny we're leaving behind, either. What about the dead people? Scary they might be, but they've been the walk-on extras in our lives for as long as I can remember. The dead people come as a package with Mrs Kinnearly. They won't be in The Dark House, for sure. There's no way Mrs. Kinnearly will be turning up on *our* front doorstep all that way away.

For weeks before we move to our new home my dad spends interminable hours alone down there. I've seen The Dark House. I hate it. It scares me stiff. I've made up my mind. I cry at the prospect of moving there. I know with the certainty that sits in the base of your gut like a tapeworm, this place is not going to make me happy. It's going to make me sick!

Dad expends huge amounts of energy transforming The Dark House into Number Eight Hughes Street. When we go to inspect Number Eight Hughes Street just before moving in, the first thing I spy as we walk up the narrow path past the garage, high up in the garden to our right, is a huge green iron A-frame swing with rigid metal arms and a wooden seat.

"Wow!" I run up the steep, slippery grassy bank and jump onto it. It takes some time to persuade me indoors. If you swing high enough, the base of the swing lifts a bit off the ground and a gentle knock reverberates through the frame, but I know it won't come out. It can't. My dad said so. I swing higher and higher, my hands gripping the thin iron rode supporting me as I make my way higher and higher, determined to get parallel with the top of the frame. But try as I might, I never quite make it. Still, it seems Number Eight Hughes Street isn't so bad after all.

I hardly recognise the house when I do eventually step through the back door. Where there'd been bare wooden floors there's now lush shag-pile carpet, walls have been papered and the paintwork is magnolia. The bedroom I'm to share with Anne is pink and we have brand new twin beds with matching bedspreads and pink curtains. Our window ledge is wide enough for me to sit on, and you can see all the way down to Mount Baths, where I'll later learn to swim and flirt. It's from there that I'll watch flames rising in the dark as the textile factory just up from the swimming pool goes up in flames. It's the most dramatic piece of spontaneous pyrotechnics I'll ever see in my life. My mother's got a spanking new washing machine, and my dad's got a garage to keep him occupied, with a tool shed next door. Peter can keep his bike dry now – essential in the endlessly cold damp winters here. And he's got his own bedroom with a green lampshade. At last he's got a room of his own.

Mam takes me to Ponty on the bus, just the two of us, and we buy a snowy mountain landscape from Woolworths to hang in the lounge. It takes ages to choose. This is a big decision. The house is nice. The snowy picture looks good. There's a new friend called Enid around the corner, and she really likes the picture. And Monkey lives a few doors down. I don't know her name. Everybody just calls her Monkey. They go to a different school, but Mam says it's best if I just keep going to my old school, and then I'll have my old friends and my new friends. Maybe life here will be OK after all.

I go back out on my swing. There's an old door at the bottom of the garden and Peter helps me unhook the swing rods and lift the door to lay it across the frame, making a *brilliant* den. Mam gives me some old blankets to hang down the sides and Dad finds me some old carpet to put inside. Life here gets better and better.

We haven't been in Number Eight Hughes Street very long when Dad goes into hospital. A TB ward. I ask Mam what a TB ward is, and she says, "Don't be stupid, it's just the name of a ward…he hasn't got TB!"

I make friends with a new girl in school, called Cerys, and my dad makes me an Andy Pandy rag doll while he's in hospital. He sews it all by himself, and Cerys says that's really clever. For a man. He's gone a long time…a really long time. And when he gets back he's thin – really thin. I think he's going to die, so I ask the dead people, "If my Dad dies by mistake and goes to heaven, will you send him back?"

Cerys says definitely they will. Definitely.

"That's what dead people are like."

I am six when Dad's in hospital, and my sister falls in love with Jeff. He's the first boyfriend she's ever had, and I like Jeff. Mam does too. I don't know about Dad, but he laughs and jokes with Jeff and they talk about sport all the time, so I think that's OK. Anne smiles a lot, and I saw her kissing Jeff, so I think they're somebody you have a baby. I think weddings are great, because the bride always throws a load of tanners for the kids to collect, and I'm really good at seeing them quick, so I normally end up with a few bob. Cerys says I might have to be a bridesmaid too, but I'm not too sure about that, because we don't have a lot of money for fancy things like bridesmaids after carpets and beds and washing machines and snowy pictures from Woolworths. The tanners will do me fine – especially if Anne throws a few extra my way. I'll have enough for sweets for weeks.

When Dad comes home from hospital he takes me up to Granny Sally's on Sundays. We go on the bus, but we don't pay because Dad's got a special card called a Driver's Pass. I like being on the bus with Dad and I think I might be a bus driver when I'm older.

Hang on, though. I can't. I'm a girl!

Today is Sunday and we're going to Granny Sally's. We're at the bus stop and Dad's smoking a cigarette while we're waiting. Behind him there's this big wall you can climb up and I'm up there playing King of The Castle. The other side of the valley I can see this massive slag heap. That's what they call some of the girls round here – slag. When I'm 6 I think they burn these girls, and when they turn to ash and soot, they dump them up on the mountain with all the rest and that's why they call them slag heaps.

"You alright?" he checks, looking up at me. We're the only two waiting. Sunday afternoon is always quiet because none of the shops are open, and most people don't go out.

"Yeah."

I shrug my shoulders.

Then my dad drops his cigarette on the ground and stops it burning - with his foot. Then he smokes another one right away. And he never does that. Not straight away. Never. But today he does.

"You sure you're alright?"

He's looking at me like I shouldn't be, but I don't know why. So I just tell the truth.

"Yeah!"

I mean, why wouldn't I be? It's Sunday, there's no school, and we're going to Nana Sally's. Why wouldn't I be alright?

"Come on," he says. "The bus is coming."

And he reaches up to lift me down in his arms. And then he stops, with my arms around his neck. I can feel his smoky breath on my face. His hair looks really nice today - all slicked back tight with Brylcreme. His eyes are twinkly blue, and he looks like he's been crying, but dads don't cry.

"You know Granny Sally won't be there today, don't you?"

"No. Why?"

And I have to wait.

"She died."

And the bus pulls up, without a sound, and the conductor opens the door, silently.

And my Dad looks at me, still in his arms.

"Is that OK?"

And I look into his wet eyes, the cigarette dangling from his lip.

"I mean, do you still want to go?"

Course I do! My cousins are still there, Allan and Susan, and we're gonna make mud-pies and play kiss-chase, like we always do. The boys hate it, but we make them play anyway. What a stupid question – course I still wanna go!

But before I can say a word I look at my dad, his Woodbine dry on his pale thin lip, collar loose around his neck…and I see him dying right in front of my eyes.

* * * *

I only see my father cry two more times in my life: the last time is when he drops me off at university.

Marriage

My father was a quiet gentle man, but I'm not sure I knew that as I grew up, and it makes me sad to say I never had the chance to really get to know him – not as an adult, but not even as a child. On only one occasion he slapped me. I'd answered back, 'given him cheek'. I never gave either of them cheek again. I must have been about eleven when I learned not to answer back. It never left me, where my parents were concerned.

The most vivid memories I have of my childhood are of my father packing a suitcase and leaving, more than once. The sound of that front door slamming turned a knife in my stomach. I didn't know it at the time, but he would go and stay at Auntie Megan's house, his younger sister. He would always come back, but I could never be sure. One minute he was there, the next he was gone – and maybe for ever, as far as I knew. My memories of that time are dominated by bitter acrimonious rows between my parents, week after week of silence, and my father being 'sent to Coventry' for interminable stretches. I only dared speak to him in secret snatches and lowered tones when he was 'in Coventry,' unsure how my mother might react if she thought I was crossing enemy lines.

"Tell your father his dinner's ready."

"Dad, Mam says your dinner's ready."

"Tell your mother I heard her."

"Dad says he heard you, Mam."

And we're all in the same room, and when I'm six I don't understand this – not one bit. I have agonising recollections myself of being sent to Coventry by schoolmates – seven, eight, nine years old – and never knowing why. Just because they felt like it, I suspect now.

Just because they could. That's what little girls can be like, I've come to realise. Boys too. Children can be very cruel. For some reason I expected better of the adults in my life. I guess most children do. But how easily expectations change.

You could see with a glance that this was mental torture for my dad, psychologically and emotionally banished in his own home. But try as he might not to rise to the bait, you could never be sure the silent hostilities wouldn't erupt into another Krakatoa at the first inadvertent fanning of flames on his part.

What on earth many of those rows were about, I have no idea. But there was one instance when I didn't even need to guess. He was called John.

Before the war John and my mother had been engaged. John's parents had spilt and he'd come to live with his grandparents in Mount. There were a surprisingly large number of broken families in Mount back then, and likewise in the sixties. Maybe we weren't out of step with the rest of the country at that time, though: two wars in less than a generation inevitably cause social breakdown. Hasty marriages, premature parenthood, young widowhood – they all took their toll on family structures.

My mother was an attractive, bubbly vibrant young woman unless our many sepia photographs deceive. And there is no reason to suspect that – except, of course, the difference between the young woman smiling broadly at the camera, full of laughter and meeting life head on, and the huge contrast with this entirely other woman we all knew as our mother and wife to both her husbands.

John became my mother's first love. His family were Catholics and my grandparents were from a long line of Baptists, my great-grandfather renowned for his lay preaching with great hwyl. It didn't take Hailio Salasio to know this match was never going to be smooth as far as the families were concerned, but they were in love. Before long their engagement was announced. My mother was deliriously happy.

But soon John went into the merchant navy, and then my mother too joined up when war broke out. She spoke very little of her wartime experiences, other than to say it was the happiest time of her life (before the marriages, before the children) but she did talk about being stationed in Belgium at one point. Our mantelpiece above the Rayburn was home to a much-treasured Mannequin Pis ashtray she had brought back from Brussels, a souvenir used far too frequently over the years by my father.

It's not easy reading a closed book, but in my mother's case the book was not only closed, but padlocked and set in resin. There was no getting close, let alone hoping to touch her, so working out why life was as it was, well…even giving it my best shot, that was never going to be a fruitful exercise. I guess she must have remained in love with John for the rest of her life. If we could run the story again frame by sorry frame, maybe we could work it out; maybe we could spot the exact moment where it all went so hugely wrong that she became a different person entirely. Maybe there *was* a possible happy ending, after all. Maybe if they had both come back to Mount, settled down, had their own children, things could have worked out for them. Maybe she had the potential to be happy. Lots of maybes.

But somewhere along the line there was some story about a young woman writing to John from Canada, and John's father waving the letter in front of my mother. And before you could say "set-up" the engagement ring was in the river, my mother was on the market again, and she wasn't to speak to John for years. That was that. Except it wasn't. Not really. Not for my mother. Not at all.

John went on to marry someone from England and he moved away. My mother went on to marry twice, both times disappointed in love, disappointed in her men, disappointed with life. Nothing her men could do was right. Nothing they *could* have done was right. Not Bill, and not Tom. Because there was only one thing that would have made it right, and that was something neither of them would ever be able to do – they couldn't be John.

But my Dad was my Dad and I wouldn't have had it any other way.

Dad

Dad was a bus driver most of my life, although before I was born he was a miner for some time, swearing nothing would ever get him back down the mines. In my young days he'd driven a pale green, brand new shiny Morris Minor delivery van for a local baker's. Those were the days when bread was delivered to your door, fresh and crisp. He carried orange juice too, and what seemed to me at the time to be *gigantic* boxes of biscuits, cakes and other delicacies on his rounds.

The back of that van smelled of freshly-risen bread and iced buns, sugar-sweet and sticky. By some measure they were the best I've ever tasted – sweeter and softer (and stickier!) than even the great and famous food halls of today. Fortnum's? Nah! Tiffany's? Get away with you! Back of Dad's Van? That'll do nicely, thank you. Were they just super-fresh, I wonder; or was I just super-impressionable. Maybe it was the sheer delight of being allowed to sit in the back of that heaven with my dad. He delighted in having the opportunity to give me something that made us both smile.

Soon after that he was driving buses, and it feels like only yesterday that he took me year after year to the Red & White Bus Company children's Christmas party. Just him and me. No Mam. No tension. No waiting for the next ballistic missile. He'd sit and have a beer with his mates in the company canteen while we kids were busy passing parcels, ripping the paper off when the music stopped, playing Blind Man's Buff and musical chairs – nearly breaking legs (chairs and each other's) as we barged each other off the seats, desperate to remain in the game. Then the highlight of Santa's arrival, weighed down with games and toys: they never skimped on their presents, the Red & White, fair does. And the very best of all came at the end - sitting not on Father Christmas's lap, but on my dad's knee, him teaching me the nonsense chorus to the old familiar Max Bygraves song: *Gilly Gilly Ossenfeffer Katzenellen Bogen by the Sea.* I didn't care that there weren't enough seats to go round for the sing-song in that canteen; I didn't want a plastic seat. My dad's bony legs did me fine. Arms wrapped around me, he'd hold me close, singing away seemingly without a care in the world. It was a far cry from the man I saw at home – relaxed, carefree. This was the man they saw at work. This was why busloads of drivers and conductors turned up at his funeral. They sang their hearts out in memory of this kind, helpful workmate. This was my dad away from Number Eight Hughes Street.

*   *   *   *

Driving buses through, around and between the valleys was a hard, physical job in the sixties – a lot of tricky manoeuvres on narrow, winding roads not made for large vehicles, and no power steering. There was one excited occasion I recall when people turned out en masse to see where a double-decker's roof had been sliced right off as a novice had driven the wrong route through Abercynon, mistakenly assuming he would squeeze under the railway bridge. Nobody'd been injured, thank god, but it was nothing short of a miracle that lives weren't lost that day. It kept the valley entertained for weeks on end.

Bus driving was notorious for inducing heart problems, combining as it did a lot of heavy upper body pressure with otherwise entirely sedentary requirements like issuing tickets. This was in the days before power steering, the days when manual gearboxes grated and ground their way around, often involving a battle of wills. It was particularly difficult after OMO was introduced: One Man Operation, the curse of the life of the bus crew. Job losses for the conductors and heavier workloads under more pressure for drivers. Before OMO there'd been driver and conductor on each bus, teamwork bringing all those benefits you read about in short introductions to management….camaraderie, shared experience, waking up in the morning actually (incredibly) looking forward to being at work. Motivational theory, I believe they call it. But OMO did away with all that. Now it was all down to the driver. And then there was the additional worry an Inspector might be lurking at the next stop, clipboard in hand, ready to mark you down as late, inefficient; to hell with the fact that someone needed a hand – a miner with emphysema, a widow with a heavy load, an old boy who didn't really know where he was going, but he was along for the ride anyway. It wasn't my Dad's *job* to help the young woman with a pram and two kids get on his bus - but he did, of course. There were lots of things that weren't his job but he did them nonetheless. When it came to the question of whether to get out of his cab and help people, passing the time of day with a pensioner out for a chat and some human interaction, or alternatively hurrying them up to make absolutely certain he was spot on time, for my dad as with many others, there *was* no question.

Yes, there were higher wages for those who'd kept their jobs, and some clippies retrained as drivers of course, but increased productivity - which is what this was all about - only happens if output goes up more than costs. OMO added a load of stress to the driver's day, while profits rose for the bus companies. Much the same the world over, of course.

The job certainly took its toll on his health. Constant antacid pills, the occasional pain in his chest which he only mentioned once when my mother told him to get an appointment with the doctor, and he didn't like doctors – they did things like put you in TB wards for weeks on end with no good cause. Shortness of breath, exhaustion: these were things he lived with daily. Life's inevitable little irritations, as far as he was concerned. That was Dad. My dad.

The union recommended all drivers invest in life assurance at reduced union rates, and my dad told my mother he was. He didn't, and we'll never know why, but it left my mother in a financial mess when he died suddenly on that fateful New Year's night. Maybe he was just rubbish at paperwork like me. But he certainly knew what it was to work hard. He took on unsocial and unhealthy shifts to boost his earnings, the early shift or late shift meaning he was rarely around at the same time as me. Then he started night shifts when the work became available. Sometimes he would do a split shift or a double-shift, back to back. That would see him leave the house before dawn and not return home before midnight. Often he worked weekends.

Constantly changing work and sleep patterns played havoc with him, and he found himself with an ulcer and admitted to that TB ward before I was seven. I wonder now whether life with my mother was easier that way, spending every moment he could behind the wheel. He would have explained it away as a mortgage needing to be paid, and wages being low. With my mother doing a series of low-paid unskilled jobs in the years before the Minimum Wage was introduced, Dad's extra earnings were undoubtedly both welcome and necessary. But I do wonder.

When he was home, Dad spent his time in the garden or, more often than not, in the garage. He made sure my swing was in good nick, he made me stilts…but then he would disappear into the carbon-caked, damp dump of a garage, fiddling with my brother's crumbling Mini or, later still, Peter's ill-fated motorbike. A self-proclaimed dab-hand at car maintenance, my father loved the challenge of keeping old jalopies alive – fixing clutches, changing a gearbox, cleaning plugs and points. He bought himself a Lambretta. It didn't work when he got it, but he spent all his free time stripping it down, part by precious part, cleaning it, replacing anything that took his fancy, then putting it all back together again. He never got anywhere near getting it to work.

He would appear for the odd cup of tea in oil-soaked overalls, hands caked with car detritus, squeeze a generous measure of Fairy Liquid into his hand, and scrub his nails thoroughly clean before filling the kettle.

Not once did I ever see him with a hair out of place, brylcremed to perfection and black as the coal he had mined in the years before he lay with my mother and made me. I think now that he never wanted that Lambretta to work. That garage was Dad's refuge. Why would he want the Lambretta fixed? He would have to find another wreck to work on! The greasy floor, air saturated with petrol fumes and Woodbine, the portable radio barely audible above the revving of knackered engines…. Saint David's Cathedral itself could not have provided greater sanctuary for my father. This was a world he understood, a world in which there was some semblance of normality, a sense of him being at least partly in control of his life. It may only have been a garden path away, but for him that garage was a million miles from the house we called Home.

Mother

I feel only sadness when I think of my mother. So much of the life she lived was obsessed with the lives she hadn't. She made no bones about the fact that if she were to have her life over again, she would have done things very differently. In particular she would not have married the men she did, and she would not have had us. No bones about it at all. I have always been desperate to make sure my son knows exactly how much he was wanted and is loved.

And yet there was another side altogether to my mother, a side in which she and I were close – very close. Parks figured big in our lives. There were rare occasions in my early life when she would take me down to Miskin Park, and then later further afield to Aberdare Park, Ponty Park. Just her and me. (Anne and Peter never had the pleasure of these trips, and pleasure it really was.) At Aberdare, a couple of miles from the poverty into which I had been born, the park was and still is a haven for all ages. We'd spend a long stretch on Saturdays, picnicking on tinned salmon sandwiches (always John West, only the best), Smiths crisps you shook the salt onto, and crisp juicy grapes from the greengrocer's on the way to the bus. She always had a plastic mac for us to sit on, and while I played on the fantastic huge climbing frame and the magic roundabout, my mother read *Woman* and did her knitting. She knitted all my school jumpers, and taught me how to knit Fair Isle and Aran, how to darn socks. Only me, though. And I'd go out in a rowing boat, waving to her on the grassy bank or a wooden bench. The boating pond is still there in Aberdare Park, although it seems smaller now if no less alluring and beautiful in its green wide-open setting. Some years later my friends and I would 'accidentally' roll the boats over, much to the consternation of the boat keeper, a terror of teenagers drenched and dripping on the bus home.

At Ponty we'd spend the entire day on a Saturday. The unheated open-air pool was (and still is, even to my adult eyes) enormous, with different sections to play in, and a fountain in the middle. Freezing at first, it soon warmed up, or we cooled down – one or the other. But either way it was bearable, and I always seemed to make a friend – as kids do the world over.

"Susan's really good at making friends," my mother would boast. "You should see her in Ponty Park – the minute she's in that pool, she's found somebody to play with."

Not exactly how it was, but it was nice to think she believed it.

Then it was the ubiquitous salmon sandwiches, more pool time and then a walk around the park, beside the river Taf, fast-flowing and dark with coal dust. Later in the afternoon the bandstand buzzed with activity as the crowds gathered to hear the Salvation Army or the colliery band. I'd play hide-and-seek with my new friend while my mother sat on the grass knitting.

We'd visit the market at Ponty too. People came down from all three valleys to Ponty market in those days. Famous it was, although it's a shadow of its former self these days.

"Come on ladies! Royal Doulton, this is. Look, sixty-piece set for three quid! You gonna let me give it away for that? *Course* you're not! I'd have to be mad to let it go for that. Look at it, madam! Feel that. Hold it – go on. How heavy is that? Is that the genuine article, or is that the gen-u-ine article? Come on, madam, tell these good ladies here. How much would you pay for that in the shop there? Sixty nicker, that's what you'd pay down there!"

We'd stand freezing in winter at stall after stall, free entertainment for hours on end – better than any air-conditioned, central-heated shopping arcade of toady. And quality it was, too. I have still got the towels my mother bought on Ponty market for me to go off to university. 1975 she bought them, and they're still as good as new. Certainly, they are – if your glasses glow pink, that is.

Then it was home for the wrestling, with a nice bit of tongue in the bag for tea – off one of the stalls in the indoor market. Always the same stall, just in the corner on the left as you headed through the market with the outdoor stalls behind you, gaslight pouring down on the butcher like the set from a Victorian melodrama. And it might well have been: who *knows* what tongue that might have been, sitting on our plates while Jackie Pallo floored Mick McManus with his Flying Lariat, bouncing off the ropes to build up speed before wrapping his arms around Mick's neck and taking his legs from right under him. My mother, my father and Granny all adored the wrestling. Glued to it they'd all be over a cup of tea, Granny in her house and my parents in ours – but not usually with mam and Dad in the same room on the same day. Shift work helped them stay apart much of the time. Right up until the final second of the final round, they'd shout at the TV screen, yelling encouragement for whichever opponent had won their favour that day. What a pity the boxing had no more success than anything else in bringing any of them closer to each other.

My mother surrounded herself with song. The radio was always on in our house. She listened to The Light Programme, later Radio 2. Whenever I was home ill from school, as I frequently was with repeated tonsillitis, she would tuck me up under a blanket on the sofa and we'd listen to Worker's Playtime while she caught up on the laundry. I can't remember her ever sitting down with me and cuddling me – it wasn't her thing. But I would drift in and out of sleep to the sounds of the radio and the lulling regular chugging of the washing machine as it went through its cycle. For dinner I'd agonisingly try swallowing a spoonful of Heinz tomato soup to Worker's Playtime, coming from 'somewhere in Britain'.

The mouth-watering, stomach-rumbling smells of Sunday roast mingle in my memory with wafts from the kitchen of Family Favourites, kicked off with its signature tune, *With A Song In My Heart*. The Christmas Special, with the forces overseas linked up with folks back home, was an institution in British households of the fifties and sixties. Ours was no exception.

And all of it was music, music, music…with the odd bit of comedy thrown in. On the radio, that was – not in real life.

And there was singing – lots of it. I joined Penrhiwceiber Junior Choir and the school choir, and my mother sang too. She sang with Tom Jones *(I Am Coming Home To You)*, Shirley Bassey *(As Long As He Needs Me)*, Frank (and Nancy) Sinatra *(Somethin' Stupid)*, Ella Fitzgerald and Sarah Vaughan. All to the radio in our small terraced house in Hughes Street. My mother sang her heart out – but only when she thought no-one was listening. The one song she wouldn't -

THAT PICTURE OF YOU

couldn't – sing along to (not even *listen* to) was Ella's *Every Time We Say Goodbye*. If it came on the radio she'd turn it off. Until John came back into her life, that is. Then she could listen to anything. Even Ella. Until he went again.

My father's favourites were classical, although he too listened to popular contemporary music most of the time. He would sneak off to our rarely-used front room (kept for special occasions, but we never had any) and he would play his vinyls on the record player in peace. I only know this because I found him there once, and he invited me in to let me hear what he listened to in his secret life. Tchaikovsky's 1812, and not just the overture; The Enigma Variations – all of them, but Nimrod in particular; Mahler's 5th, and especially the Adagietto, the theme from Visconti's *Death In Venice*: these were the pieces he loved most. But it was *Danny Boy* that made him cry. The tune, *Londonderry Air*, has done the same to me ever since. I still can't sing the hymn *I Cannot Tell* without fighting the swell of emotion that cracks my voice.

> *I cannot tell how all the lands shall worship*
> *When, at His bidding, every storm is stilled,*
> *Or who can say how great the jubilation*
> *When all the hearts of men with love are filled.*

My father never experienced the stilling of storms, nor that jubilation which comes with the full heart of one who loves and feels love in return.

Re-fusing

I don't know what the fates must have visited on my mother along the way to make her behave the way she did, because she always insisted to her dying day that she'd had an idyllic childhood. The youngest and fairest of four, her three big brothers adored her. So too did her doting parents. Granny, a seamstress, made all her daughter's clothes by hand, sewing late into the night after the children had been settled, the kitchen cleared and things prepared for the next day. Sat at the pvc-clothed kitchen table, she would thread that Singer sewing machine with matching cotton, the foot pedal rising and falling to the sound of my Gransha snoring in the armchair next to her, by the glow of the fire.

"I was always the best dressed girl in Mount. Granny made sure of that."

My mother painted the rose- and-sepia-tinted picture of lace sewn exquisitely around the collar of her precious Sunday best dress, woven as delicate as the wings of a damsel fly; of the finely embroidered flowers around the sleeves of her blouse; of the satin lining of her red coat, gleaming as it caught the winter sun. All made by hand; all made with love.

And my Gransha spoiled his little girl too – with the first egg his much-loved hens laid in the morning, still body-warm, thoroughly washed to remove the last speck of chicken shit; the first crisp peas to sprout on his allotment, sweet as the pineapple chunks Granny kept in the walk-in larder for special occasions. A small plateful of peas, all for his little girl to eat raw out of the shell, the sweets of her day.

So what was it that went wrong? And when? Was it the dream, so close she could taste it like honey but tossed away into the swirling murky water along with that sparkling engagement ring? A life with her John in a two-up, two-down in Miskin or on Aberdare Road, snatched so violently from her by that letter from Canada, never read but waved like a victory flag right in front of her face? Was that it? Years of bitter disappointment and growing disillusion with first one husband and then another, who could never be what she wanted, could never be the man she loved, could never be John? Was it that? Or was it that she was afraid of being happy? She, like so many little girls (and maybe she above many, given the immense love and happiness her parents shred) had grown up with the myth that marriage would make her happy. So she had married, once, and been thoroughly miserable – depressed even, I believe. Then she had married a second time and found it no better. After my father's premature death at the age of forty-nine with my mother only two years older, she had a great deal of life ahead of her. With three children and soon after a number of grandchildren, you'd think she might have finally found peace. But having been unhappy in marriage she was now positively suicidal being alone. I can only put it down to depression, and we all tried endlessly to get her to recognise it and seek help, all to no avail.

But whatever it was, I wish I knew. Because what our family had to bear was living with someone who, through her own suffering, committed others to a path littered with the shards of her broken dreams, never daring to put a step wrong for fear of the devastating bloody consequences. Somehow, though, I can't believe it made her any less unhappy that others suffered too. Or did she maybe not notice?

It's hard to know which of us three children suffered most. Not that it's something you do - quantify these things. It doesn't matter in any case. It doesn't mean a thing. Not then; not now. We all suffered. In different ways, to different degrees, we all carried her pain.

Anne, as the eldest, carried all the responsibility: from a very tender age, right up to our mother's death at the age of 81, it was Anne who picked up the baton and ran with the role of carer for all of us. As good as half a century ago, when my mother headed off at some ungodly hour before dawn to work at AB Metals and I was still in junior school, it was Anne who got me up, making sure I had everything I needed, trying to get this whingeing child to eat something for breakfast. Readybrek was all I'd consider - and 'consider' was quite literally all I did sometimes, pushing hot milky oats around my bowl with a cool sulk. No straight-forward case of shoving a bowl of cereal under little sister's nose and letting her get on with it in our house. It was a serious case of every trick in the book to cajole, plead, persuade. Perversely (or maybe somewhat predictably) if Pete asked, I was more inclined to oblige.

Then it was out of the door in coat, scarf, mittens, hat, wellies (on appropriate days, with school shoes carefully wrapped in a plastic bag, to change when I got to school) - whatever it took to get me properly ready, it was Anne's responsibility to make sure it all happened. Homework book in my little brown satchel? Yep, that would be Anne's responsibility. Cough medicine before leaving? Yep, that would be Anne's responsibility. Dinner money in my pocket? It had better be. Month after month and year after year - and all those duties lovingly deployed for the good of what I can only think of as this little brat of a sister. Extraordinarily Anne doesn't see me that way, and she insists she never once resented that gruelling morning routine. More than a bit irritating, that, Anne! Just as well we love each other.

In the early days Anne then had to get herself off to school, on the bus to Abertaf, down the valley. A young woman who had learned prematurely that she should follow the rules, she was terrified at the thought of being late, and almost without fail she was on time. When she did fail, there was one particular female teacher who'd especially taken against her (and that was like taking against Mother Teresa – you just *didn't*), finding every opportunity to put her into detention or mete out some other random routine punishment. She could be guaranteed to be lurking like a trapdoor spider, ready to cast her web over this defenceless young girl. What Anne could not realise at the time was that this woman had an issue with girls in general, not just her, but my meek and gentle sister must have been the absolute epitome of everything this sharply dressed career woman despised. Later when she was to teach elsewhere, her relationship with a particular sixth-form boy was reputed to be much warmer than anything we ever observed with her own sex. She and Anne were like chalk and cheese – she the ripe camembert: she stank, as far as we kids were concerned.

Anne has vivid recollections, hardly surprisingly, of a stormy night around the time I would have been six or seven, when it seems only she and my mother were at home. Peter would like as not have been up at Granny's, and I might have been up in our bedroom, I suppose, or else have been at Granny's too, or one of my friends' houses nearby. Either way, to all intents and purposes it was just Anne and our mother in the house while rain lashed against the windows, propelled by violent winds. I imagine Dad must have been at work; driving that night would have been treacherous. Buses caught the wind side-on as they headed out along the bleaker, more open stretches of the valley, drivers soon working out where to brace the vehicle for the gusts.

This night the winds were so severe all the lights blew. In complete blackness our mother called Anne downstairs. Mother knew where the fuse box was but she, like me to this day, had an irrational fear of electricity. I believe firmly that sometimes you just have to feel the fear and do it anyway, so I can handle repairing fuses if needs must. But this wasn't a philosophy my mother shared. If you were scared enough of something, you got someone else to step up to the breach. Obviously. So by candle-light she set about getting Anne to fix the fuse. Anne was thirteen and had never seen a fuse box in her life.

This was the early sixties, when Anne and our mother found themselves in this dark place, under the stairs in candle-light, face to face with a fuse-box that neither of them could fathom.

"You'll need something to get up on."

In the dark Anne drags a dining chair through from the lounge, which doubles up as a dining room. The only other room, the parlour, is kept for special occasions.

"What do I do?" Nothing before her makes any sense whatsoever, and she's terrified, the agitated dust rising and catching her throat.

"How do I know? You can work it out when you get up there. Go on."

Faced with the option of arguing with my mother or climbing onto that chair to try to work out how fuses work, Anne raises her young foot and places it on the brown vinyl seat cover, pulling herself up and taking care not to bang her head in the ascent.

"What do I do now?"

"How do you expect me to know! Open it up."

Unable to see much by the light of the quivering candle down below her, Anne feels along one side of the cold metal box, then the other, catching her finger on the sharp handle. She flicks it up, and the heavy grey cover drops down, falling only just above her head. Craning her neck, she stretches as high as she can, trying to see if there are instructions in the box. Nothing she can understand. Her eyes are barely able to make out the contents, so small is the pool of light surrounding her mother's face like something out of a Georges de la Tour painting.

"I don't know what any of this is." Anne's voice is almost inaudible, terror strangling her words.

"Well, work it out. Here – there's a fuse. You'll need to replace one of them."

Anne pulls out what she thinks is a fuse, applying her trembling fingers to the wire; her heart beats so loud she's sure mother will hear it. If she does, Anne fears she will be in even more trouble for making a fuss. She determines to do the best she can, but with hands shaking uncontrollably it's difficult pulling out the first fuse. Unwrapping the new wire from the packet she has been handed by Mother, her trembling fingers twist and prod it into place, ready to be popped back in. Calmer now, she pushes the fuse back into position in the box. The next thing she remembers is a loud bang, and she is on the floor, heart racing faster than she's ever felt in her life.

When she'd suffered rheumatic fever as a small child, Anne had almost died, and had been left with a serious heart murmur. She'd become used to frightening palpitations and arrhythmic heartbeats. But she knows this is something altogether different. This is gut-wrenchingly terrifying. Her whole body shaking from her head to her toes, she picks herself up off the floor, her head throbbing as if she has been hit by a mallet.

"Come on. We need to sort this out. Get back up there."

Anne almost glances at her mother for a moment in disbelief, but she daren't look her in the eye. Unable to believe her ears she stops for a moment, trying to make sense of what she has just heard. Did her own mother actually insist she goes through all this *again*? Didn't she *see* what had just happened? Was Anne *imagining* all of this – could this be a nightmare she'd wake up from any moment now?

"I'm going to die," she thinks. "If that happens again, I'm going to die."

She knows it with a total conviction that's new to her. Here, under these stairs, in the dark with her mother at her side, her life is

THAT PICTURE OF YOU

probably about to end. And once she has accepted that, she feels an incredible calm come over her. She has spent thirteen years being punished one way or another for being alive, for breathing. Now it was about to stop. This was the answer. She didn't need to be alive. There was an alternative. And for the first time in her life, my sister realises there is at last a way out.

Boldly this time, she climbs up onto the seat, ready to accept whatever her fate will be. And as she does so, an enormous sense of peace descends on her.

Peter's way of coping with 'family' life is to make himself as scarce as possible. He heads up to Bryngolwg each day after breakfast, up above Granny's house. He pops in to see her every day on his way to the secondary modern, and often he spends his evenings there in the sanctuary of the one significant adult in his life who has always shown him real love and affection. Granny and Peter are soul-mates. Still they are - even though she's been one of the dead people for more than thirty years now. Other times he cycles – up to our Auntie's house, off to the coast, down to Cardiff even. As a young teenager he's happy to do fifty miles in a day, alone or with friends.

When we moved to Number Eight Hughes Street our mother had clearly been worried that ten-year-old Peter would refuse to leave Granny's, and if he had it would have reflected badly on her and my father. But all that was said was, "You know Elwyn (*his friend*) can come down to play in the new house, don't you."

"Yes?" It seemed a strange thing for her to say.

"That's alright then."

And that was the end of that conversation. Clearly he'd be moving without a fuss, she'd established.

In the evenings, Peter walks back up to Granny's with a big faux-leather bag holding two plates with her supper in between and the whole thing wrapped in newspaper to stay warm as he climbs Mount Pleasant Terrace. It's as good an excuse as any to escape the dark house, now more brightly decorated but forever dark in our souls.

With the passing of time Anne finds herself packing me off to school first thing in the morning while mother has already then started her day at AB Metals down the valley. The components made there were stamped 'Made in England' for export, causing a good deal of resentment it seems. Eventually though the stamp was changed – to 'Made in the UK'. Not much better, but since the main thing that defines being Welsh is *not* being *English*, it was better than nothing.

My father meanwhile makes his way at ungodly hours off to the buses. Then my sister heads herself to work in Durbin's insurance company as it was back then, as Bill Durbin's secretary. She enjoys the new-found taste of independence, saving her money for a new coat, new shoes, a trip to Paris with Jeff. She has begun to see another longer-term way out, a life beyond the confines of The Valleys and Hughes Street. Anne likes her job. She is good at it – very good – and it gives her self-esteem. She is treated with respect there. But most of all it gives her choices.

As for the breakfast rigmarole, I really cannot imagine she enjoyed that one iota. But she did it well. No, she did it far better than 'well'. She did it brilliantly. She has always had a natural instinct for home-making and caring for others. When it came down to looking after me, though, she wouldn't have dared do any less than she did. I was, and I remained, that blue-eyed girl, the princess. I was the baby; but more importantly I was the sole progeny of our mother's second marriage. I can't imagine what must have gone wrong in the first, but go wrong it most clearly had. Now the second was faring no better.

I'm nine and I've been chosen to sing in the concert on St David's Day with David Batley. Now, there was very little that was more embarrassing for a nine-year-old than standing up in front of the whole school and singing –except, of course, standing up in front of the whole school and singing with a boy. That absolutely was the worst – unless you had to stand up in front of the whole school and sing *Oh no John, no John, no John, no!* with a boy, kitted out in wedding garb! And where on earth would we find a wedding dress to fit a nine-year-old me, in any case?

Well, that's where 'Auntie' Meg comes in. Auntie Meg lives a few doors away and luckily for me she's a dab hand at sewing. Not only that, but she's thrilled at the chance of making me a wedding dress. The only problem – well, the *main* problem - is that we don't have the kind of money you need for material to make a really *nice* dress, and Auntie Meg insists on making a *really nice* dress. She isn't going to put her name to anything she'd be ashamed of.

"That's alright," she announces. "I've got an idea!"

And that's how I come to find myself being measured up for a really *really* nice wedding dress made out of white crepe paper - with a veil to match, made from an old pair of net curtains. It's the business! And no, my worst fear doesn't come get fulfilled – it neither rips nor tears. Nor is it transparent.

And that's when I learn that if you take on another persona, you can get through *anything*. Close your eyes, pretend it's happening to someone else, and just get on with it – whatever it is. Great for performance nerves; even better for real-life dramas, I'd find out some years later. Maybe not recommended if you want a well-grounded sense of who you are, but there we go. It worked as a survival strategy. Never mind 'fright or flight'. Just cover your ears, close your eyes and sing, *'la la la la la!'* loud as you like!

The wedding dress is a triumph, and the concert a roaring success. Getting in to that crepe paper dress without tearing it to shreds is a feat in itself. Auntie Meg has designed if brilliantly with flappy bits here and bits to tuck under there; it even seems to stretch, but surely not! No doubt she'd sewn it on the bias – a little technical know-how from Granny coming out there – but whatever her technique, she's excelled herself.

Granny is impressed when I take it up to show her. "Ooh, bewtiful! She's a dab hand at sewing, is that Auntie Meg! Do it with her eyes shut she could!"

I wouldn't want to risk it, personally. Needles, and all that.

So…David Batley and I stand in the wings until the headmaster, Mr Lukey-Davies, sends a signal through to Miss Davies who's playing the piano, to announce us.

"And now boys and girls, we have a special song for you sung by Susan and David!"

The applause starts and little voices chatter about who 'Susan and David' might be, when he and I walk out onto the stage. We're meant to be holding hands but neither of us is very keen on this and somehow we manage to forget. I am convinced I am *actually* going to forget my words, and my heart is racing so fast I fear the words will come out at triple speed, but it turns out fine and we sing a blinder. The applause is fantastic, and I can sense even then that I could easily become addicted to this as we now finally do hold hands to take our bow. I even manage to get both on and off stage without my net-curtain veil falling off, which I regard as one massive triumph. Hmm. Yes, I certainly think I could get used to this performance stuff. It's even better than doing it for the deeply adoring Granny and poor old Mrs Kinnearly.

My only real interest in junior school is beating Simon Farley. In everything. He and I are joint top of the class. In English I can tell a verb ("a doing word" Mr Lukey-Davies taught us – that seemed simple enough, we were *doing* things all the time) from an abstract noun (things you couldn't see, touch, hear or smell – like feelings) as easy as imagining happiness. There you go, both in one phrase. And Welsh, a foreign language to us, comes easy to me. But Maths is our real battle ground. Simon is very good indeed at Maths, and I love it. I'd learned algebra for fun at the age of eight, solving simultaneous equations to pass many a boring Saturday afternoon when Enid couldn't come out to play; for my nine-year-old brain trigonometry was the most thrilling puzzle in the world.

Maths opened up a whole world of certainty in my otherwise deeply precarious existence. I've seen this in others, too. At the age of eight Bert was brought from Holland to live with a new stepfather, speaking not a single word of English as he arrived here. An intelligent child unable to communicate by usual means, he taught himself advanced maths from the enormous Encyclopaedia Britannica he found in his new house. He determined to make sense of this exciting new world opening up before him - a world in which his "real" father Peter trotted the globe as a famous jazz band leader; a world in which his new dad had grown up as a child of the British Raj with all the baggage that entailed; a world in which his mother insisted her two boys, after spending a year in a children's home, construct an entirely fictional backstory which didn't expose her as a foreign divorcee.

They say things happen for a reason. I don't think so, somehow. I'm not sure that can be said about the constant rows and hostilities at home while I was growing up, any more than it can be said of Bert's odyssey to a foreign land in which he found himself walking through an airport gate labelled "aliens". But what I *do* think is that each and every one of us has the capacity to take control of our lives (at some point) and make sure that things are *made to have happened* for a reason, which is something different. And then even when we think the job of making sense of our past is finished, it's still open to so many interpretations.

Years ago I made time for what I suppose we'd call traditional women's crafts – knitting (sorry Kaffe Fassett!), dress-making, and eventually embroidery. I bought a canvas some ten inches by twelve, a range of embroidery yarns, and a picture I wanted to copy in wool – Vincent's *The Sower* – then I began to reproduce it, freehand: no sketch on the canvas, no plan of how to section it up. (I must add, at this point, that I am no artist.) I started with the bit that caught my eye – the tree trunk, unsurprisingly – and just began sewing, one stitch at a time. It involved an extraordinary amount of *looking*, focusing on the direction and length of each individual brush-stroke, trying to mimic it to perfection, the subtle changes of colour becoming increasingly apparent as I studied in minute detail every square centimetre of that genius's masterpiece. The bark alone had so many shades to it that I was forced to go back to the craft shop several times, adding to my ever-widening range of threads. I ended up with almost an entire basket of browns, greys, purples and greens. I became so engrossed in the detail of each miniscule part of the picture that for a while I lost any sense of the whole. But that attention I gave to, and the time I spent on, just one section produced something so fine, so beautiful, and so true in its own right that when I stood back and looked at what I saw before me, it took my breath away. Did *I* do that? Was that me? That's remarkable!

And isn't this what we find we do with our 'selves' – taking just one part of us, working and reworking it and seeing where it takes us? Memory plays a crucial role in this. When we re-member (literally, putting the bits back together) we don't at first see the whole, not during the process of working on one aspect of our selves. We remember discrete episodes, and not even in any particular sequence. We remember events, episodes, one by one as they come to the surface. Then we create a narrative that weaves them together and brings us to where we are now, at this precise moment in our lives – to who we are right here, right now. But when we return to these memories again, then again, and when we share them with others who were there, others who remember the same episodes but not in quite the same way, we add another thread to our tree trunk, another brush-stroke to our picture, weaving their narrative through ours, in and out, now visible, now not. That's what makes the picture: the interweaving of our own narrative with those of others.

We cannot change where we've been, how we got to be *here*. But we *can* reframe things, touch them up a little, repaint a section or two and set some great foundations for the brush-strokes we will come to add in the future.

What I now believe is that things don't necessarily 'happen for a reason' but that we can retrospectively *and* in moving forward give reason and purpose to that which has happened. And this making sense helps us to cope with even the most troubling periods of our lives. But before I understood this I found other ways to cope with the traumatic life in our home: learning Maths was one of them when I was at junior school. Later, sex would take over the role when I naively mistook it for intimacy and love.

Auntie Meg

It's funny now I think of her, the woman who made my wedding dress, who was a neighbour down the street: Auntie Meg didn't come across as exactly what you might call a domestic goddess, and yet she clearly loved sewing. She could cook a damn good Sunday roast, too. But apart from that she wasn't your run-of-the-mill housewife. In fact, if you believed my mother her natural habitat would be walking the street corners down in Tiger Bay when the boats came in. Nothing near the truth, of course, but there was such a jealousy on my mother's part that there was an entire fantasy world created around this tall, attractive woman who looked after herself.

My mother couldn't cope with the fact that Auntie Meg wouldn't be seen 'without her face on'. If the rent man turned up before she'd taken her curlers out, 'back-coombed' her hair and slapped some lipstick on, she'd rather be turned out in the street in arrears than caught out pallid and in a hairnet.

Mrs Malaprop of The Mount, Auntie Meg suffered from "terrible condescension on her windows" in winter. And when brown sludge spewed out of her taps after a water shortage one summer, she complained to anyone in earshot. "Ridiculous, it is! That Water Board's spent millions putrefying that water, and look what they go and give us! Daylight robbery it is!"

Auntie Meg decided in her fifties to learn to drive.

"That'll be so she can go off and see her fancy man thinking nobody knows where she's going!" Irony not being a word in my mother's lexicon, the bitter jibe was too much to resist. Auntie Meg's supposed lifestyle – supposed only by my mother, it seemed - was beyond the pale. She was even going to drive! A Woman, for godsake! Driving a car all by herself? Shameful!

My mother never learned to drive of course; no, it just wasn't a woman's place behind the wheel – and for her generation that was pretty much true, I suppose. It was a man's job to get you around the place, just like it was a man's job to know how electrics worked in the house, or how to organise life insurance. So Auntie Meg was something of a maverick. And it was a clear enough sign of loose morals if any woman lavished all that money on driving lessons for herself - secret assignations, that's what it was about, according to my mother. Going places and meeting people behind everyone's back, that was it. What other reason could you possibly want with driving yourself about the place?

So Auntie Meg, rather late in life, signed up for driving lessons. A dozen. Nothing if not optimistic. She wasn't what you'd call the most naturally gifted driver by all accounts, but to be fair it's not so easy picking up new skills at that age, and in Mount there were particular hazards in trying to get around on four wheels. Turning through ninety degrees into Clarence Street after the near-vertical incline at the top of Mount Pleasant Terrace for instance, was enough to drive anyone to distraction. But if you were unlucky enough to have to stop at the brow and let a car, a bike, a pedestrian cross the top, and then do a hill start on the bend, you could burn your clutch out in one fell swoop.

Auntie Meg did find hills a bit of a challenge, even after she had passed her test on the fifteenth attempt. Getting out of her car late one night in their sharply-inclined road – having been out with her fancy man, no doubt, in my mother's eyes – she had walked away without pulling the handbrake fully on. Clearly distracted – by memories of his seduction, my mother would have concluded – she'd gone in and shut the door, making a good strong cup of tea. Milk, two sugars. Then she'd turned off the lights and gone to bed in the room next to the sleeping Harry's.

Luckily nobody had been injured as her car had inched down the road, across the lane and down the steep bank into the back gardens below. It caused quite a kerfuffle getting it out, believe me.

The narrow main road snaking up through the valley posed a bit of a challenge too. There was a particular occasion, on one of her tests, as she drove up through Abercwmboi – testing at the best of times, but the degree of hazard raised by the presence of parked cars on the far side of the road, and road works on the near. Undeterred, or more likely oblivious, Auntie Meg boldly went where no ordinary driver would dare. Oncoming cars having priority and indeed oncoming at speed, she had gripped the wheel steadily and kept her foot down, heading down the middle of the road as bold as Boadicea in her Ford Anglia.

"Are you sure?" The instructor gripped the dashboard: there were no dual controls in Auntie Meg's car.

"Sure about what?"

"There's enough room?" His voice was now an octave higher as he closed his eyes and braced himself.

"We're fine!"

The sound of metal on metal.

"What the hell was that?"

"Don't worry," she replied brightly, "...it was only a digger." It had gouged every single panel of the car. She went on to fail the test on more than the several minors she'd already clocked up by then, and never could understand why she hadn't passed: it was only a digger for goodness sake! And whose business was it if she scratched her own car, anyway – nobody'd died!

She did finally manage to get her licence, albeit leaving her examiner with the impression she was a bit dim. "What's the first thing you do when you pull off a motorway, Mrs Thomas?" Pencil poised to tick the box – or more likely *not* by then.

"Well, funny you should ask that, because I don't know about you, but I always have a good strong cup of tea. Milk, two sugars."

"Mrs Thomas…"

"Now Harry, he likes a coffee, but I can't be doing with all…."

"Yes! Thank you, Mrs Thomas. Well, you'll be pleased to know…"

And in my mother's imagination she then leaps on the examiner and gives him what for – right there at the door of the test centre. In full view of the whole of Ponty.

"She'll have been up to no good with that instructor, that's what's been going on, if you ask me. That's why she keeps failing – so she can keep on carrying on with him."

Er….I don't think so, somehow.

SUSAN J BEVAN

Christmas

Mother didn't speak to Granny for years after we moved out of Clarence Street. None of us had a clue why not. Yet every day she would send one of us up with a hot dinner for her, and never once did she object to us spending time at Granny's.

"Where you off to?"

"Granny's."

"OK. Will you take this up for her?"

Nor did she ever bad-mouth her. But she adamantly would not make that ten minute walk up the hill to see the mother who'd given her that 'perfect childhood'.

One December Mother told us to invite Granny for Christmas Day. We three could hardly contain ourselves. We'd asked for years if she was coming for Christmas. Loving her as dearly as we did, we'd spent too many years witnessing the loneliness, the isolation she suffered, her world gradually closing down to whoever came in through her front door. Always open, too rarely entered. But never once did we hear her complain. She wore a smile day in, day out, however great her pain – and just how great it must have been is hard to imagine.

"What's the point in crying about it? Won't make it any better, will it! Does no good being miserable on top of it all. A long face gets you nowhere, gul."

Life was a daily struggle. In those often bitter mornings before double-glazing and central heating, she would climb out of bed after another inevitably pain-ridden night, struggling to pull on some clothes against the chill and damp. The first job was always to light a fire. Even in summer she would rake out the grate, haul in a metal bucketful of coal from the small cwtch outside the back door (Peter would have made sure there was enough brought up from the big cwtch under the kitchen), and start rolling up old newspaper to get the fire going. With the cinder from the day before and kindling she had chopped herself on a log at the top of the steps, she'd get a flame started before you could spit. Then it was up with a sheet of newspaper across the fireplace, held in place with a long iron poker, and she'd hobble off to fill the kettle in the bosh. In no time at all it was aglow.

The sight of those flames blazing behind that paper, roaring louder and louder as the colour and heat intensified, was as much a thrill to Granny at her old age as it was to us growing children.

And she was fearless with fire. I'd nervously watch it licking the paper, turning a small patch of it brown, and then just as it was about to set the whole thing alight she would whip it down to reveal an inferno filling the hearth. The heat was enough to send me flying to the sofa for respite. Then it was on with the kettle, and warming the teapot. Every day without fail started with a good strong cup of tea laced with Johnnie Walker's, and it kept her going right into her eighties. Living out her final sad months in a nursing home, it was easy to see what that morning routine had done to keep her alive. It was downhill from the day she moved – left with no option after taking a dreadful fall down those fourteen hard steep stone steps, breaking ribs as she tumbled towards the garden, helpless. Alone in the house and with none of the neighbours hearing her cries for help, she'd dragged herself back up into the house and not even got anyone to call for a doctor. The only sign of any injury was a slight wince when she moved suddenly, grabbing her ribs. Peter was forced to press her into tell him about the fall. She didn't want to make a fuss, she'd said; she'd be alright. She must have realised at that moment that there was no way she could stay any longer in that house alone, and she'd have been terrified of being put in a home. It was clear that not one of her children was willing to take on the responsibility of looking after their mother in her declining years: they'd escaped Clarence Street and waved it goodbye along with the woman who'd loved and raised them, all getting on with their own sad disappointed lives. There'd been no looking back for them.

That fall was the beginning of the end for their mother.

So we three children were thrilled when Granny was invited for Christmas Day. Although we said nothing to each other at the time, it turns out we all secretly hoped this might be the start of the process of her moving in. Then she could be properly looked after, like she deserved. We children were more than willing to pull our weight. After all, she had certainly done more than her fair share for us.

It was hard to tell who was more excited on Christmas morning, us or Granny. Despite us pleading that she should come early, she agreed Peter could pick her up at twelve. At least she was going to be with us for the rest of the day.

Anne and I got the table ready, attending to every detail as if the Prince of Wales himself were coming. (He was popular in Wales at that time, and later to be invested shortly before his twenty-first birthday.)

Granny lovingly took out of the drawer her very best brand-new blouse, with silk-covered buttons and delicate lace collar, and her favourite-coloured turquoise cardigan, packed away in tissue paper for a 'special occasion'. A special occasion was usually when her youngest son Uncle Tom made his annual visit or, very much more rarely, John or Idris, the eldest two, came to see their mother – Jack from Coventry, Idris from North Wales. I saw Idris and his wife twice in my life, Jack a handful more times. Not one of her children was what you might call attentive.

Christmas Day dawned and Peter drove up to collect her, arriving spot on time. Granny was at the door waiting, radiant, handbag under her arm. She locked the door behind her. It must have felt very strange: she hadn't walked more than a few paces down the street for years, not even crossing the road to the houses opposite. She would wave across, her neighbours calling, "Hallo Ruth! How you faring?"

"Could be better," or "Middling. You know." That was as bad as she'd admit.

Getting in that car was difficult with her crumbling bones and buckled legs. That spine was under enormous pressure as she carefully twisted and eased herself down into the passenger seat. "Ooh!" She had to take it slowly.

"You OK, Gran?"

"Yes boy, I'm fine. Just caught me for a minute." She took a deep breath.

Peter gently closed the car door behind her; she wouldn't have been able to twist to reach for it, and certainly not able to pull it. She'd washed her hair - another gargantuan feat involving kettles full of water carried from the fire to the bosh, then drying her hair in a towel and 'coombing' it to perfection. No wonder she'd said twelve o'clock. With this severe disability she'd have taken the entire morning to have a full wash-down and get her Sunday Best on. With not a lock out of place, her hair glistened like fine silver-white thread in the winter sun.

Arriving at our house she found me, the youngest and least controlled, quite literally jumping up and down with excitement. Her 'wriggle-pants' as she'd called me when I was little. (She regularly inspected me for worms, finding them once or twice and bending me over and removing them with toilet paper.) I could barely contain myself today. And there she finally was, lifting her foot up over the front step and walking slowly into our house for the first time, for Christmas Day! After all those Christmases alone in Clarence Street, she was here: back with her family - back where she belonged.

"Peter, get your Gran a drink if she wants one," our mother called from the kitchen without so much as a glance in our direction.

That's how it started and that's how it continued. She had laid down the ground-rules in one fell swoop. *She might be in our house because you children all went on and on about it, but don't expect me to have anything to do with her.* We worked out later it must have been my father's suggestion. She'd gone along with it but she made it patently clear she wasn't buying in to any of it.

Over Christmas lunch our mother sat at the opposite end of the table from Granny so they wouldn't have to speak to each other directly, and making sure she'd pull her cracker with me. Not once did she even look at her own mother once – not one glance, no single look of recognition. Not before nor during nor after that long, awkward meal. With each forkful a deeper gloom descended, engulfing even us most stoic of grand-children.

By early afternoon Granny's heart was in pieces. She knew exactly how you made a home, precisely how to make people welcome. Even the much-despised rent man and whipperine felt welcomed as they stopped by to pass the time of day with Granny. So she knew full well when she'd overstayed any welcome there might have been in the first place. By mid-afternoon there was no damage left for my mother to do. Our Christmas was a wreck.

"I think it's time I got back, Peter," our Gran said softly. We hadn't even got as far as the Queen's Speech as I pleaded with her to stay.

"I don't think so," she said, offering my mother the chance to contradict her. "I think it's time I was off."

Her paper hat was still on her head as she walked out of the door. She never looked back.

Leaving

Things were never right between my parents, but by the time I was ten they were at an all-time low. My mother treated my father with contempt, clearly not bothered if he came back or not next time he would leave. The atmosphere was so bad the marriage looked unlikely to last no matter what my dad did to try to pacify his wife. The relationship had crumbled beyond repair, and he had no idea how on earth they'd found themselves there, and what he'd done wrong.

The truth was that John had been back in my mother's life for several months now. He'd happened across her by sheer chance on one of his rare visits to Mount to see his family; his wife had died of cancer he told her, as he and my mother stood spellbound on the pavement a short distance from our front door. Even at that age I could understand how devastating that must be for John and his daughter. These were the days when the very mention of 'The C Word' was all but forbidden. Rare though the disease was back then, few could name anyone who'd survived it. Indeed, the fight against breast cancer suffered decades of stagnation because the word 'breast' couldn't be mentioned in public. Even in a doctor's surgery it was 'the chest area'. Cancer was a word that filled the heart with terror.

So yes, I understood they'd been hit by tragedy - even as a child I understood the devastation of cancer, never spoken until someone had passed away. "She's got...you know." So of course it was a disaster for John and his only child to lose the wife and mother in his family. But for my family too it was a disaster - for all of us. Except my mother, that is. Here was her exit strategy from a second unhappy marriage. Her intention was to secretly leave the family, leave Mount, and take me with her. Only me. Just the two of us. This way she wouldn't even have to face the music with my father. She'd be hundreds of miles away, safe in the arms of her former fiancée – with the man she should have married all along. Anne and Peter would be left with my dad, their step-father. They had a difficult enough relationship with him already; this could only make things far worse. He would be bereft and no doubt angry, as one is in the grieving process. But that was his problem. She wasn't missing out on this - possibly her last - chance to be happy, to be with the man she'd always loved. Maybe she could magic that ring back out of the river now, at last.

When she met John in the street that day she didn't invite him in – not even John crossed our threshold. Or maybe *especially* not John. Maybe she daren't. Soon though she was passing messages via his sister. Then it was letters – from her direct to him, the replies through the sister. Then a phonecall, and another. Finally they'd met up in the sister's kitchen. The first secret assignation for me to witness, sent to play in the front parlour with his daughter Sharon. We eyed each other up, neither knowing what to make of what was going on between our parents. She talked funny; her accent wasn't like anything I'd ever heard. And she was older than me – only a couple of years, but that felt like a great deal back then. I didn't want to be her friend. I didn't want to play with her. I wanted to be out of there, home with my dad and brother and sister.

Soon there were clandestine visits to a phone box several streets away. If Dad was on a late shift trying to get the mortgage paid off, it was easy; she would just go. There was only me to be accountable to, and I was her confidante in any case, so there was need to explain. I was a child, after all. Why rights did I have? And didn't I want her to be happy, and live in a big house, in Essex? How could I say no!

"I'm just going up to phone John, OK?"

"OK."

Of course it wasn't OK.

"Now, you know what to say if Dad asks where we've been, don't you."

"To the shop."

"Yes. Oakland Street, right?"

"Right."

She was bursting with life, taking my hand in hers and almost skipping up those streets like a schoolgirl - a teenager again, engaged to the one and only love of her life.

She was cunning too. My mother could have run a cracking resistance outfit in the war, if she'd had the mind to. There was absolutely no doubt we'd pop in to the shop in Oakland Street and buy some milk on the way back, laying down markers. A converted front room in a semi-detached house, the shop was indeed somewhere you'd easily hang around half an hour waiting to be served, the counter dispensing every titbit of news, gossip and hearsay. But tonight we were served swiftly before making our way back home. 'Home.'

Walking into the house after these betrayals always left me feeling like sick and sad. I hoped my dad would be in the garage or somewhere, anywhere but here. It shouldn't be like this.

My mother's plan was to start a brand new life with John and his 'lovely' daughter Sharon. I'd met her just that once. We'd be happy at last, my mother insisted, eyes aglow. No more shouting. John wasn't like Dad. Essex she said was a nice place to live – not like Mount.

I liked Mount. Mount had everything I knew. Mount was the only home I'd ever known. Mount was Wales. Essex was England. We hated the English.

I coped by trying to pretend the seemingly inevitable wasn't going to happen – forget about it, ignore it, and if you do this long enough and hard enough it'll all just go away. Burying my head in the sand, if you will, but I didn't see it like that then. So faced with the threat of leaving Mount, my Dad, leaving my brother and sister, Granny, my school, my friends, and everyone and everything that was familiar to me – in short, my life – I ignored it. And here we were, still in Mount. Ignoring the threat did seem to be an effective strategy. Or so I thought.

But my mistaken conclusion that the dash for enemy territory had been shelved was exposed for what it was when one afternoon my mother took me secretly into her bedroom while Dad was at work. Opening her underwear drawer, reaching under her white pants from M & S and her white bras from Castrees in Oxford Street (Mount, Wales, not London, England), she pulled out a chain with something dangling on the end of it. It was small but hefty and glittering gold.

"Look what John sent me!" She sounded like my friends when they got an unexpected Valentine's card. It was as if I was her best friend. But I wasn't. She was my mother. This was my father she was betraying, not to mention Anne and Peter.

"But don't tell Dad," she was conspiratorial, like a twelve-year-old.

In her hand, I could see now, was a small gold watch on a chain. I'd never seen a watch on a chain before and it struck me, as no doubt it did her, as highly exotic. Gold-plated, its sparkling sapphire face was studded with what looked like diamonds.

My feelings at being drawn further into this web of hers were totally contradictory. An uneasy thrill that my mother trusted me with her most intimate secrets battled with the guilt that literally made me sick. The pit in my stomach told me no good could come of this. But her delight at sharing something so seismic as this affair was evident in everything about her. She was radiant, years younger. I'd never seen her like this.

Even at eleven I knew why this was our little secret, why it was me she was sharing this with: there was absolutely no-one else she could have involved in her plan. As far as I could see, she didn't have a single friend – at least, none she ever talked about. Oh, there was a friend she'd had in the WAAF in the war, and a very occasional mention of someone from work, and then there was the woman from Aberfan. But she never actually saw these people. She never saw anyone. No-one ever came to our house. No-one at all. I can't recall anyone ever stepping over that threshold, except us five and a couple of friends of mine. And Anne's boyfriend Jeff of course, who was like family member number six anyway. Oh, and Granny of course, that once.

"Take it," she beamed, handing me the watch. "Have a look."

I looked. No matter how hard I looked, it was still a watch on a chain.

She reached back into the drawer.

"Look what else he bought me."

She gently flicked open a locket, compartments begging for a photograph, a lock of hair….something they could exchange when they were finally together again, launched into their new lives - lives that included nothing whatsoever of what constituted our family life here, in the valleys. Nothing of home.

"Aren't they lovely."

There was no option. "Yes."

I felt nausea rising. The urge to grab them both, hurl them through the window and smash them to smithereens, or trample them into the baby-blue fluff-flecked nylon carpet, the urge rose in me like bile. Sure I was about to be sick, my face reddening and head throbbing, I struggled to find words.

"Can I go over to Enid's?"

Enid Thomas was my best friend and lived across the road. She wouldn't be in Essex either.

"I've packed my case," my mother said, replacing her precious things where they wouldn't be found, "and I'm packing yours in a minute before Dad gets back. I've got train tickets already. We'll be off in a few days."

I said nothing.

"OK?"

"OK."

"Isn't it exciting! You'll have your own room. That'll be nice, won't it."

I liked the room I shared with Anne. But it wasn't a question, anyway.

"Can I go over to Enid's?" I was about to be sick any minute.

"I'll put the cases under my bed, because nobody'll be under there, so if you need something I've packed, just ask me. But don't let Dad hear you."

"OK."

"Or anybody else."

"OK." She closed the drawer and leaned on it, still with that smile on her face, her mind clearly far away.

"OK."

"So can I go?"

She has forgotten.

"Go where?"

She wasn't even listening. "To Enid's." Please god, let Enid be there.

"Come back for tea at six." She looks so happy, so young - so alive.

"OK."

Thank god, Enid's there. So is her brother Paul. He's fourteen and sent me a Valentine's card this year. His friend Tom's around too. Enid's got a crush on him. The boys want to play 'Nervous' with us in their cluttered back parlour, dark heavy curtains keeping out much of the light. This is a new game for me. We usually play Subbuteo. The boys explain. 'Nervous' involves two 'teams' each with a boy and a girl. Enid's brother wants me on his team and it becomes clear why as the boys explain the rules. The two teams each find a hidden place in different parts of the room. Not difficult: you can hardly move in here for the junk. Empty suitcases, bags of old clothes; there's a piano under all of it somewhere, but you'd probably have to climb over a mountain of old toys, sledges, bedding and old rolls of wallpaper to get there. So we have to find a secret spot, which may or may not involve construction, tents or blankets. It's important, they insist, that the teams can't see each other. The game starts when the boy places his hand on the girl's knee.

"Nervous?" he whispers to her.

The rules only allow for two answers. Even to me at that tender age that's obvious. "No," entitles the boy to move his hand a seemingly random number of inches up the thigh, only to ask again, "Nervous?" Another "No," continues the game until his hand is in your knickers. At that point, if the other team are still negotiating, you've won, and the boy gets to kiss you for as long as he wants, tongues and all, with his hand inside your drawers. Apparently it's a prize for both of you. Personally I don't get it. It transpires though that the losing team do exactly the same, which I think removes any notion of competition - but the boys don't see any moral imperative to explain this at that precise moment. They're just keen to get started.

If, however, at any point you reply "Yes," then it's your turn to put your hand on the boy's knee, and continue (assuming he doesn't get nervous!) until his predictably rock-hard penis is firmly gripped in your sweaty hand. From then on, you just follow instructions from the boy - generally communicated in grunts - along with the kissing. Well, it's a cheap game for poor kids, I guess!

I'm a bit nervous about starting the game at all, to be truthful; but Paul tells me that if we don't play, he and his friend will tell his parents it was *me* who made the game up. I'll get sent home in disgrace, he says (but not so eloquently – *"you'll be in a shitload of trouble"* was, I think, more like it) and I'll never be allowed back over to play with Enid again. This is my first taste of sexual coercion, and I'm not even a teenager yet! The prospect of being sent home to my mother right now, disgrace or no disgrace, is more than I can stand. I climb over junk, lift my skirt and bare my knee. I learn not to say no. I am ten years old.

SUSAN J BEVAN

John

Then somehow Dad catches a whiff of duplicity. He's not daft. That bloody John! It's *got* to be. He's back in her life, he realises. Call it sixth sense if you will. Or maybe somebody tipped him the wink. Either way, desperately trying to avoid confrontation, he pieces the jigsaw together without saying a word.

One fateful bleak mid-winter night he secretly follows my mother and me up to the phone box. He keeps a safe distance as he trails us, but he really needn't bother. Once we're out of that door, my mother never looks back. All she can see is that new life ahead of her, and my Dad certainly won't be part of it. Why would she want to look back?

Up Bush Road we go, up past Ford's corner shop where we do our regular grocery shopping, fruit and veg on display outside, even at this time in the evening. Up around into Thomas Street, taking in the smells of the best 'scraps' in Mount from the corner chippy. Up the steep street, past the terraced houses, TVs audible through single-glazing and net curtains, dinner plates from Ponty market on nylon laps on nylon sofas; and finally, breathlessly, left into Gladstone Street, level ground at last. Down to the far end, where the phone box stands next to a small plot of waste land, a rough path leading down a gully between the gardens.

In she goes. Hiding around the corner at the junction of Thomas and Gladstone Streets my dad hides and watches, distant as he could ever be, as my mother tries to dial him out of her life.

Outside the phone box I hop from one foot to the other and back again, teeth gritted against the chill. I'm cold right through. The whirring of numbers being dialled – lots of them – then chink, chink, chink.

Coin after coin of betrayal. Chink! Another coin. Another deceit. Chink! Another secret, another lie. Trying to stand far enough away that she'll think I'm not listening, in truth it doesn't seem she's bothered even if I am. While she's on the phone to John, I don't exist – not as a real person with real feelings, not as a daughter. Nothing exists. Nothing outside that red box. Especially not that crushed man at the end of the street, hiding around the corner from the truth he knows he will soon have no choice but to confront.

I shiver to the bone in the dark damp night. John. Not quite her lover, I think now, but still in the thrill of the early chase.

The cold starts to work its way through my jumper – I haven't worn a coat because we flew out of the house while the coast was clear, and I thought we wouldn't be long. But now ten minutes are turning into twenty, and still she's laughing away. Now and then she goes all quiet. I guess they're smooching down the phone, the cooing and calling of love birds; there are some things you don't want to hear from your parents – not even to each other, but *definitely* not to the 'other man'.

I look over at the lights in the windows across the road, the houses up above us with their little front gardens sloping down to the grey stone walls dropping down to the pavement.

Somewhere my dad must be frozen too.

How did that feel? How was that for him, that moment when all those niggling suspicions were confirmed? Watching. Watching his wife, the mother of his child, the mother of two others still only youngsters themselves. Watching me, frozen out by my mother, shut out in the cold but woven into the fabric of that cloak of deceit of hers. How did he feel, my dad?

It's still there, that phone box. In 2013 it stands on the same spot. I called home from it last time I went to Mount. It still works. Right at the end of Gladstone Street on the left-hand side, where you get a clear view over to The Tumpy – or Twyn Bryn Buchan, the 'mountain' across the valley, standing at a thousand feet according to Miss Ellis in our Geography lesson but actually more like fifteen hundred – its smooth green patches of grassy field nestled between the Forestry Commission's ubituitous evergreens. Behind us, a crow's nest overlooking the valley is Aubrey's bar and restaurant, hanging there in the night sky like a castle in the air. Perthcelyn, "The Lost

City" as it's known locally, ironically twinned with the majestic Machu Picchu, about as unidentical a twin as ever there was.

I would have been anywhere else but there, that icy night.

Then the call is over, and she comes out all smiles, and I notice she has put lipstick on, especially for the call. She'll have to wipe that off before we get home!

Down Thomas Street we go, the descent much quicker than the breathless climb, down and down to what's waiting for us at home. We pick up a pint of milk on the way home to provide the alibi.

Usually when we get back my dad's still down in the garage. But tonight he's not. The light is off. There he is as we walk in, sitting in the corner of the lounge, legs crossed, cigarette in hand. Everything feels oddly quiet, eerily still.

"Cor, they don't half talk in there. You could be there all night just for a pint of milk!" She puts the milk on the mantelpiece to demonstrate we have indeed been to the shop, then takes off her coat and shoes, keeping her eyes fixed on the task in hand as she slips her feet into her slippers. I peel off one boot, then the other, turning away from my father as I bend down.

"It's perishing out there!" she shivers.

Still he says nothing – he just sits there in his chair, legs crossed tightly, staring into the middle distance as he drags long and hard on his woodbine.

"I'm going upstairs." I say, hanging my coat up.

"Susan, put the milk in the fridge," my father says firmly.

My mother takes off her coat and hangs it up under the stairs. "OK."

I do as I'm told. He has never given me orders like this before, leaving most details of domestic life to my mother, but tonight there is something in his voice, in his eyes - and I don't like it. Is he packing his bags again tonight? Will he come back this time? I shut the fridge door very gently, overhearing in hushed tones, "Where have you been?"

"What?"

I can see them through the door. My mother's sitting down with a catalogue. She orders lots of clothes and kitchen things from catalogues. When I was little I used to cut out people – whole extended families – along with everything you needed for a perfect life – fridges, beds, cars, garden sheds – and make my own play things to keep me amused for hours on end. (It gave me the option of choosing an ever-changing glamorous model as my paper avatar, changing the husband and kids at the drop of a hat.)

"Where have you been?" He looks her straight in the eyes for the first time now.

"To the shop. I told you. Oakland Street. To get milk." She calls to me in the kitchen, "Haven't we, Susan?"

I come in and glance at my father, desperate. His eyes are still locked on her.

"Yes," I answer weakly. I know already there is no point continuing with this charade.

"No you haven't. I followed you. And don't drag Susan into this." He is very calm.

"Well, that's a sneaky thing to do behind somebody's back!" She whips the page over.

"Susan, go upstairs," he says, his colour rising as he stubs out the woodbine in his new ashtray that swallows up the butts and spins them round.

"Get ready for bed," she adds, whipping another page over as I leave the room and close the door *almost* tight behind me.

And once more I find myself sitting at the top of the stairs in my pyjamas and dressing gown, straining to hear. Hearing them is easy, I have learned. Catching what they say, although I can imagine the gist of it, is impossible. What lies am I being drawn into now? What will I be told to say or not to say next? And what if I get it wrong? Whatever happens, it'll all be my fault.

I draw my knees up under my chin, and the tears fill my eyes until they spill onto my cheeks, first one eye then both. My chest burns as I try to suppress everything I feel. Please, just stop this. No more. Please!

Later when I walk through the sitting-room to get a drink of milk before bed my father is sitting, still, in his chair in the corner. He is quietly sobbing. Through the kitchen door I glimpse my mother standing at the sink, arms folded tight, jaw set hard. I swear that if she'd had an iron bar between her teeth she would have cracked it in two. In that instant I am suddenly aware I have never seen my mother cry. Tonight is not going to be the first time. I'm stuck in this room, and my feet won't take me to the kitchen. I might as well be pinned to the ground. I am ten years old.

"Can you see what she's doing to me, Susan?"

"Ignore him, Susan!"

I am frozen to the spot.

"Can you see? Just look! I love your mother. Can't she see that? I'd do anything for her. And I love you, too. And she does this. *This*! I don't know what more I can do. I swear to god I don't know any more."

When I'm back in my room and I'm drinking the milk, blankets up tight under my chin, shaking from head to toe and barely able to breath, I'd swear that milk is sour.

Birdsong

He whistled, my father. He whistled like a bird, and if you asked anyone who knew my dad what they remember of him, it would have been his whistling. He could have whistled for Wales. A beautiful, pure sound with a trill unmatched in anything I've heard since.

It's late June. I am twelve. Dad comes home from a late shift around eleven, insisting I get dressed. I've never seen him so animated, but I'm all ready to head off to bed when *Parkie* ends in a minute.

"Come on, Susan. Get some clothes on." He's grinning, cigarette hanging in his hand. He takes a drag.

"Why?" I look at him, bemused.

"Dave's got the bus down by the pub. Come on, get a move on - we've got to be quick. He should be in the garage locking up by now."

My mother looks on in with a mixture of disbelief and disdain. She doesn't move a muscle, except her jaw.

"She's ready for bed."

"That's alright. Keep your pyjamas on, then. Just get something on top."

So I throw my jeans and a jumper over my pyjamas, and grab a jacket from under the stairs. I can't find my shoes.

"Slippers will be alright." He smiles in my mother's direction. "You coming, love?"

"Where?"

"It's a surprise."

My father loves surprises. I wish I'd been able to give him some in return. Premature death is a dreadful and indiscriminate thief.

"I'm not going out this time of night!"

"Aw, come on. It's lovely. It's still warm."

"No. And that's final."

As we pick our way down the garden path in the dark I catch a whiff of his breath. He's had a beer after his shift, as usual. Maybe that's why he's so animated. They do say the odd drink removes inhibitions and the real person breaks out – the one locked away by those throttling constraints society imposes. In my father's case it didn't take anything as big as a societal meta-lock. My mother throttled him single-handed with her tongue. It was no wonder he sought solace in a pint glass most nights before heading home.

Being on a bus around midnight is an odd experience back in the days when pubs turn out at half ten and 'Last Orders' really does mean drink up, get out and push off home. At a time when there were fewer cars on the roads in any case, we're a lone vehicle for most of the run down the valley. With just the three of us on the bus, my dad perches on the windscreen ledge, fag in hand, chatting cheerfully with the driver, his colleague and friend. I can see this is his natural environment, his shoulders set so low I'd have failed to recognise him from behind - none of that tension holding his body taut as a wire at home.

Travelling backwards through these routes he knows so well, his body moves gently with each twist and turn, held in an easy, unlikely equilibrium.

I watch as he takes a long, relaxed drag on his woodbine, blowing smoke rings into the air. I'd thought this was magical when I was smaller. Now it only speaks to me of heart disease and lung cancer, no longer filling me with that simple pleasure in seeing his display of his art.

I hope he didn't take my cool response as a rejection of him. I was rejecting what was, amongst other things, ultimately to kill him so young.

"Come up here with me." He senses my disapproval maybe.

The bus should have been in the garage a long time back, now, but Dad has cajoled Dave into running us the few miles down to

Abercynon. Soon he would have to turn the bus in and get some kip before picking up the crews for the early shift.

I stand close beside my dad, his arm around me, preventing me falling as the bus lurches through ninety degrees, down the steep hill towards Abercynon Juniors. How strange it is to be this close to him. Intimacy isn't a word in the emotional lexicon of our house. Touch isn't a sense we indulge in when it comes to our family – not any of us. I've never seen my parents hold hands, even, let alone hug or kiss.

I can only imagine that when my mother found her husband dead on that New Year's morning, that this must have been one of her greatest regrets – the lack of intimacy in their lives. It was as if they lived in silos, the two of them, popping their heads out now and then to check up on the other one and then disappearing back down again. And yet even to her dying day, she still kept us all quite literally at arm's length. Hugged, she'd have no idea what to do with herself, only coping by patting you firmly on the back throughout, in much the same way professional wrestlers do to signal they're conceding the round.

The bus pulls up in an isolated unlit layby behind the Navigation Arms at the butt end of Abercynon, just where the sprawling valley opens up into the black void of Cilfynydd Common, with its slag heap looming above.

"OK. Here we are."

My dad is first down the steps and out of the door, even before the engine is halted and lights switched off. I'm next, wondering what on earth's going on.

"Where are we going?" I pull my jacket around me. June it may be, but it's hardly balmy.

"Here, but you need to keep quiet. Just stand completely still."

I whisper, close to him now. "What do you mean 'here'?"

"I mean here. Just here. Wait a minute and you'll see. Well, not *see*, exactly, but…"

We wait a minute. And we see nothing. Not at first. The only sound is the light breeze tickling the trees. If it wasn't for houses across the valley, windows twinkling against the blackness of the hill, we might be the only people on earth tonight.

My father puts his finger to his lips to signal silence, his other hand indicating we shouldn't move a muscle. We are barely breathing.

And then she comes - the three of us standing there like lost souls, as she comes to us. Quiet at first, distant. Then closer… "Shhh!" ….and closer still. A whole melody of rich powerful notes, like nothing I have ever heard. We stand, in awe. And I look at my dad. His face looks up to the sky, searching the trees, searching…eyes eager to catch a glimpse. The flesh falls softly on his thin face, his hands in his driver's uniform trouser pockets, a cigarette dangling from his lips. And for the first time I notice that he is beautiful. Handsome, yes. But more than that: he is beautiful, and it radiates from him. There is a tenderness and a vulnerability that I have rarely seen in a man as he watches, and listens. Totally transfixed by this small bird that none of us can even see in the darkness, he is in another world – one of peace, and calm.

We stand for maybe ten minutes like that, maybe fifteen. And then she sings. She sings and she sings. And then he whistles. My father whistles his rich powerful melodic notes, talking to the bird, and she answers. He looks at me as he whistles to her, and I want to hug him but something holds me back. It's not what we do in our family. I think now, did he want to hug me too? Was that whistling to me, his eyes meeting mine, as close as he could get now that I was growing up?

And then she's gone… first a short distance away, then altogether. It's silent again, apart from a far-off car on Cardiff Road.

"Wasn't that worth it?" he says, putting his arm around me as we head back to the bus, lights already on and engine revving to go. Dave is keen to get his head down and get some shuteye.

"What was it?" I ask, feeling closer to him than I have words to describe, and enjoying his arm over my shoulder.

"A nightingale."

That night I catch a glimpse of my dad's soul - free, melodic, soaring high above the toil of his everyday existence in Number Eight Hughes Street.

Late

In secondary school I discover modern foreign languages, and we are introduced to the theory of music. I fall in love with my French teacher (from afar and in secret) and I'm overcome with excitement when I'm taught to read an orchestral score. (Thank you, Mrs Brace!) By the time I was to reach my final year, I will be awarded Gold Prize in the school eisteddfod for a four-part hymn composition I'll submit under a nom de plume, *Griselda Sludgebucket*. Mrs Brace was astonished to see it was me going up to collect the prize. I'd kept my passion for composition heavily under wraps. But I'd grown up with music all around me. Granny had taught me the old war songs in the outside toilet, and I'd pester her to let me perform them for her and Mrs Kinnearly, using the step between the kitchen and the living room with her walking stick in my hand and a hat that had belonged to one of the men in the family. I'd perfect my act while they waited patiently behind the heavy ruby velvet curtain I used as my stage drapes.

"You ready yet, bach?"

"Nearly!"

Then my dramatic entrance to my captive smiling audience.

Tip-toe through the tulips
In the garden
Won't you pardon me
Come tip-toe…

We don't move to England. We don't move at all, although my mother keeps talking about moving house to a 'better' part of Mount. So it's worked. I ignored the threat of moving, and it hasn't happened. I wait and wait, but days turn into weeks and we're still in Mount.

As weeks turn into months, still we are in Wales. We've gone nowhere. It seems John has all but disappeared off the face of the earth. He is never mentioned again. Fleetingly I wonder if he's dead, and I really don't care if he is, except that my mother will be utterly devastated, and it's also not a very charitable thought so it doesn't come guilt-free. But eventually I forget there'd ever been any mention of living anywhere else but Mount.

But forgetting quite so completely doesn't happen overnight. It takes time. It takes practice. By the time I'm thirteen I'm trying to forget all the misery and strife at home by seeking solace in the arms of older boys. I'm not sure I find solace, but I certainly find sex. Again. You don't have to be P D James to work out how to find sex as a thirteen-year-old girl. But I'm sure this is the real thing this time, not just a grope in someone's back parlour. He's a few years older than me, and it's clear how far I have to go if I want to keep him. And then I discover it's really quite easy keeping my mind off all the stuff I'd rather not think about - at least for fifteen minutes at a stretch. Foreplay didn't come into it.

By fourteen I've been around the block, and I find I'm forgetting more and more of the domestic strife. By fifteen I really don't think about the rows at all, because now I've got other more pressing things on mind. I'm busy checking morning after morning to see if my period has arrived yet, trying to pretend it really doesn't matter when it hasn't.

Getting hold of contraception as an under-sixteen back in Mount in the early seventies was practically impossible. You certainly wouldn't have gone to the doctor in a month of Sundays, and there was no adult around who I trusted enough to speak to. By now Anne had left Mount to live with Jeff in Plymouth, where he'd landed his first teaching job. They were married on her twenty-first birthday, sending photos home to us in Mount. Peter was often out on long cycles or up at Granny's, and in any case I wouldn't have wanted to talk to my brother about my sexual antics! There was a Family Planning centre in Aberdare some four miles away, but my boyfriend's mother was a nurse, and even if she were not to be there, the odds were stacked against me getting in and out without seeing *someone* I knew. And Mount, as I've said, wasn't somewhere to keep anything secret for long. So going on the pill was out of the question, and I couldn't persuade Terry to use condoms. It was all about timing. And to be honest, my rhythm was never much cop back then. His can only be described as non-existent.

First I tell myself it's just one month I've missed, and that it's likely to be connected with the weight I've lost: I'd been on a strict diet. I'd always struggled with breakfast, as Anne had been unfortunate enough to discover early on - so that was one meal out of the way, at least. Then one Ryvita and a spoonful of cottage cheese for lunch, and no carbs for supper – shifting weight that way was easy. On Sundays I just drank carrot juice, no solids, and I found that if I combined that with a good long walk up and over the mountain, I could lose a few pounds fast enough. My hair was falling out by the handful now though, and my new nickname at school was 'Weed' after the skinny little weed on Bill and Ben. But that was the price you had to pay to look like the models in *Jackie*.

My mother takes me to the doctor, though, insisting I'm looking 'peeky'. He gives me a tonic to boost my appetite. My appetite isn't the problem. I'm hungry most of the time, but less so by the day – which I decide is a good thing. I pour the tonic down the toilet.

After another month I tell myself it's just another diet month, but I won't even contemplate stopping the diet because I'm losing weight really effectively now. Looking at the models in my magazine I wonder whether there might be a career to be made in modelling. I'm five foot six which is pretty tall in the valleys, and while I'm not 'beautiful' I don't regard myself as 'ugly' ugly. My skin is good apart from the occasional blackhead but my teeth aren't perfectly straight, which I think might count against me. My boobs are a good size though, which always goes down well. Maybe…? Nah!

I know periods can stop when you're on a diet, so that'll be it. It's a price I'll have to pay for looking good. Anyway, there's no point worrying until I get to next month now, because I've missed this month already, so there's no point thinking about *that* period any more. There's nothing I can do, in any case. And there's *no* way I'm telling my mother. Absolutely no way! I could write to Anne, but she'll only tell Mam. Then *she'll* make me go back to the doctor. So I might as well forget about it for now. And as for being sick in the morning – well, that doesn't mean anything either. I'm sure I'm throwing up before school just because I'm trying to force some breakfast down. Just the idea's enough to make me retch. Anyway, I'm fine once the day's going and I've eaten something at break (usually an orange, if I can manage a whole one), so that's OK then.

Another month, and I'm convincing myself it's my rocky relationship with my boyfriend that's throwing my body into turmoil. I haven't told him I'm missing my periods, because he won't want to know anyway, the way things are right now. I've been with Terry over a year now and I *think* I know him well enough...but something's not right, and I haven't got a clue what. I can't believe he's two-timing me, and in any case he keeps saying he loves me. But it's just not right with him and me.

Terry's a year older than me, and he's left school already – after his O Levels, it was. He earns a bit here and there, but I don't know exactly where, or what he does. Last Saturday he said he couldn't see me because he was going to see a film. I said I could go too. I mean, it's *Saturday*. We *always* see each other on Saturdays.

"It's in Cardiff," he says.

That's more than an hour away by bus. That's a *long* way. We usually go the pictures at Ponty. That's only half an hour.

"That's OK," I say, tossing my long hair back.

"I'll be back late because I can't go until after work. You'll have to be in by half ten."

"Sod that! I'll be late. I can sneak in."

I know my parents don't bother waiting up for me.

"I haven't got any money to pay for you."

We both know my pocket money won't stretch to this, but I don't really believe he can't pay for my ticket for the pictures if I get the bus down.

"I can pay for myself," I lie.

"Suit yourself."

He's going straight from work, and he doesn't know what time he'll finish, because he might have to do overtime. There's no way he can tell me because we don't have a phone in our house. (He does in his, because his father was some big noise in the pits before he suddenly dropped dead a while back.) Anyway, as long as I get there early enough, I can just wait outside the pictures.

"Which pictures is it?" I ask.

"No idea."

"When does it start?"

"No idea."

I find out where it is, and then I find out it starts at eight. Cardiff's twenty miles away, and this is a big outing for me. In the seventies it takes about three hours on the bus and I usually only go there once a year, Christmas shopping with my mother.

So I turn up at the pictures. I've had to buy a single ticket for the bus, because I haven't got enough money for a return. And I wait. It's the first time I've ever gone to Cardiff on my own, and as we wind our way down through Abercynon, Ponty, Treforest and beyond, I try hard to remember where we usually get off the bus. But I can't picture Cardiff, now – well, I haven't been there since last Christmas, and it's early December now, and bitterly cold, even on the bus. Will I even know when we get to Cardiff, I wonder. But of course I will. Everybody'll get off, if we get to the end – and at least I remember what the bus station looks like. I'll be OK.

As it happens, I recognise the stop where I need to get off. The pictures isn't far from here, which is good. I don't want to get lost and not be there when Terry turns up.

It's raining when I make my way through the capital. And perishing cold. The streets are still buzzing, with crowds still milling around, arms full and bags heaving with presents. Only a few weeks left now. I wonder what Terry's buying me for Christmas.

I turn a corner, and there it is, exactly where I was expecting. The Odeon.

The film starts in about half an hour now, so I wait outside, stamping my feet against the cold. It's getting through my gloves, my jeans and even my woolly hat. The hat's got plaits down the side so you can do it up under your chin, but it looks better when they hang down. Mind you, it's so cold now I'm tempted to tie them up anyway! Even foot stamping's getting me nowhere. I watch the minutes tick by, rubbing my hands, slapping my arms. It's really freezing now. And it's nearly eight.

He can't have gone in without me seeing, can he? No, he'd have had to walk right past me, and I've been here for ages, watching out for him. I'd have seen him! But the film starts in a minute. He must have gone in – must have passed me. When it got really busy, maybe.

Shit! It really is about to start now. I'm pacing up and down. If he's in there, I need to get in there *now*...but if he's not and I buy a ticket...I mean, if he's decided not to come for some reason, and if I buy a ticket now, then I've got *nothing* left to get me home. Next to nothing, in any case. Shit, shit, shit!

I start to get in a panic now. I could end up down here in Cardiff all night. Not just that, but nobody knows I'm here, and I haven't got any way of letting anybody know. Shit, I've really done it now. Where would I sleep? I can't stay in a shop doorway. I'd freeze to death in this. Jesus! A shiver goes through me. I'm very afraid, suddenly.

And then, charging down Queen Street, there he is! And he's on his own. There *isn't* anybody else. He's not two-timing me!

"Terry!" I call.

He doesn't hear me, but I'm running up to meet him now. Breathless and beaming, not least of all with relief, I'm by his side with the cold air creating a smoke screen between us as I lean in to kiss him. He dodges me.

"What are you doing here?" He's not happy.

"Coming with you! To see the film. I said I would!" Still I'm smiling.

"You know I can't pay for you."

We charge back along the street, turning into the entrance now. He's clearly determined to get in for the start.

"That's OK. Look, I've got money."

And I have. Just enough to pay for the ticket, and some coppers left over, but then not enough for the bus back.

"It's up to you."

And with that he turns to the ticket booth. No queue now. The film will have started.

"One please."

"Adult?" asks the girl in the booth, smiling at this good-looking youth.

"No, I'm still in school," he lies.

"Come off it!" she laughs, flirting with him. She thinks we're not together.

"Aw, come on, gorgeous!" he says, and she coyly hands him a child's ticket and some change. He really has got the gift of the gab! Anyway, he's gorgeous himself. And with me.

The Odeon really is an impressive place – not like the cinema in Ponty. I'm so excited. Plush velvet seats, Terry sits on the end of a row. I squeeze past him to sit by his side.

He loves the film. I hate it. I don't care. I just sit close by, trying to hold his hand. Soldier Blue is reviewed as one of the most brutal films ever to come out of America. I can barely watch at times, but at least I'm there with Terry. I spend half the film just gazing at *him* because I can't bear the violence on the screen. I'm fine with that, though. I'd probably do the same even if I was enjoying it, to be honest.

As we head for the bus the icy Cardiff night is busy, with pubs pouring out and crowds heading wrapped-up for the last bus of the night to be heading up the valleys. I'm more than aware how late it is as we walk up around the edge of the castle, to the bus-stop where already a long queue has formed. The thought even crosses my mind that we may not get onto this bus. I wouldn't be surprised at Terry suggesting we sleep on the streets in Cardiff – it would be his style – but I know exactly how much trouble I'll be in already if either Mam or Dad is still up when I get home. They won't let me out for a week. And if I stayed out all night, that would absolutely be the end of it: my mother'd involve my father, which she'd only done on a couple of occasions in the whole of my life, and then they'd blame Terry. They'd stop me seeing him, I know.

No, we just *have* to get onto this bus, whatever it comes to. And as for what might be waiting for me at home if either of them *is* still awake...well, I'll have to deal with that when it happens - *if* it happens. Right now there are more immediate things to worry about – like how am I going to get on this bloody bus with practically no money.

I don't tell Terry how worried I am because he's a working man now, and I'm just a schoolgirl and I don't want him feeling he's outgrown me. I felt pathetic enough following him all the way down here tonight, like a lost sheep. The last thing he needs is me whimpering about how late it is and what trouble I'm probably in, on top of everything else. He's hardly spoken to me all night as it is. But it's almost eleven now, and I'm supposed to be home by half past ten. It's a two-hour journey home at this time of night, because the bus stops absolutely everywhere, and this is the very last one. I'm suddenly very aware that I'm just fifteen years old.

Terry gets on the bus first, flashing his ticket in front of the driver and going to sit straight down, towards the back of the bus, up above the wheel arch. I go through my change again in the vain hope that it might have multiplied magically in my pocket. The coins are barely enough to fill my hand, and there are no notes amongst them. This isn't going to get me far.

"Terry," I call, "have you got some change? I haven't got enough."

He doesn't move in his seat, where he has slumped down ready to sleep, his hat pulled down over his eyes, knees up on the back of the seat in front.

"Terry?"

"Are you getting on or what?" The man behind me is tired and wet. He looks like he's had a few as well. I'm not arguing with him, but I don't dare get off the bus to let him past; I may never be allowed back on. Then I'd be on the streets in Cardiff on my own all through the night. *Ar hyd y nos*. It can be a rough city, I know - like most others, I suppose. But it's definitely not a place to hang out on your own as a young girl. And now that thought crosses my mind, I'm getting *really* scared.

I look desperately at Terry again, and then at the driver. It takes real willpower not to cry, but I can't. I really cannot cry.

"Can I just talk to…."

He nods me past and I head up the bus to try to get Terry to be reasonable while crowds pass over their readies to the driver, and pour onto what is now becoming a very full bus indeed, with twenty or so people standing in the aisle. He pulls his hat back off his eyes.

"I told you – I haven't got any money. I've just used my last quid. I *told* you! Look! I'm not lying."

He goes through his pockets, pulling out a few paltry coppers. I head back to the driver, desperate. I am scared rigid now.

The driver's looking really fed up, at the end of his shift and the end of his tether. So too is everyone else. The last person is just squeezing on, and the windows are already running with condensation.

Every seat is full, and people are packed tight in the aisle. The stink of beery breath is rank as I find myself up close and personal with some big, heavy blokes and women soaked in cheap perfume.

The driver's got a schedule to meet, and there could be an Inspector at any of the stops on the way. It's more than his job's worth to hang about messing around with me. But he also knows he'll be in the firing line if he's found to have let someone on without a valid ticket. I know this from my dad.

"I'm really sorry…" I start, and I look at him again. I know him. I know his name, and I know he's a friend of my dad's. He used to be one of Dad's conductors in the days before OMO. He's no more than ten years older than me, and we've talked to each other loads of times when he was on my dad's bus. But I daren't say anything because he hasn't, thank god, recognised me. If he did, he'd tell my dad I was in Cardiff tonight, and that I was out at midnight, and that I tried to get on without paying. Then I really would be in trouble.

"How much have you got?" he asks, fed up with the whole rigmarole.

I sift through my pathetic handful of coins and hold out my hand, shaking.

"How far can I go?" I ask, tears stinging my eyes, swallowing them back.

"Not far. Where you trying to get to?"

"Miskin."

"Miskin!" He sighs and looks out of the window beside his cab, starting the engine. I can't see his expression but I can hear him sigh.

"OK. Give me what you've got. I'll call you when your money's run out. Go and sit down." He rams the gear stick into second, and releases the handbrake.

I sit next to Terry, who pretends to sleep all the way home; so do I, praying the driver might forget me when we reach the end of the copper trail.

With half an eye I keep a watch on the stops, trying to work out if I know my way home from where we are now. For a long time I've got no idea at all where we are. Please god let him forget I'm here. Please God! I swear I'll start going to church. I'll do a charity walk and raise money for starving kids in Biafra. Anything…just don't let him notice me. Please!

Then I start seeing familiar places. Ponty, Cilfynydd. Please, not here. Whatever you do, don't drop me here: I'd be terrified walking the two miles across bleak, deserted Cilfynydd Common on my own at night under that black slag heap. Don't drop me here. Please! I'll do anything, god! But we end up speeding past the dark expanse without stopping.

I wipe the condensation away again. We're nearly there! Abercynon, Pontcynon, Tynt, Penrhiwceiber Colliery. I could do it from here! I could walk this. Fifteen minutes it would take. Penrhiwceiber Hall. Then we're there. At the bottom of Bush Road, outside Miskin Post Office. Oh, thank you, God! Thank you!

The bus pulls up at the stop where my dad told me about Granny Sally dying. It's still raining, as it has been for the whole journey. I'll get drenched running up Bush Road – but who cares! As I stand up to make my way to the front of the nearly-empty bus, Terry looks like he's asleep. Maybe he is. I won't wake him.

I brace myself for a tirade from the driver. I must have paid for about five miles of that journey. I've been on the bus for almost two hours now. It's nearly one o'clock in the morning, and now I'm starting to think about what I'll face when I get in. But first, the driver. I skulk my way to the front, and stand beside him, trying to face the other way. Maybe he's forgotten. Probably not. Anyway, I reckon I deserve whatever he throws at me now. The bus slows. Travel-sick at the best of times, this is not the best of times and I fear I'll throw up over him when he starts laying into me. Trying to keep my eyes on the floor, I wait as the bus pulls up alongside the pavement, wait for the door to open and the cold air blow in. Maybe I can slip away before he notices it's me.

"Er," the driver says, not letting me get away with it that easily, "young lady! That was a really dangerous stunt you pulled tonight."

"I…"

"You make sure you've got money home next time you go out with lover boy."

"Sorry."

"Now get on!"

"Thank you."

"Straight home now."

"Sorry. Thank you."

Terry doesn't even look as I step off the bus. Crying with relief, I run up the dark road and through the tall garden gate, closing it quietly and locking it behind me. I pray everybody's in bed. I brace myself in case they're not. Up beside the garage, past the swing and the new extension where my father's installed a bathroom and indoor toilet. The house is dark, no lights on anywhere. I sigh as I open the back door silently and creep in. My heart is thudding furiously, and the urge to cry is overwhelming, but all I want is to get into bed before I wake anyone. I'm late – so very, very late. Nearly four months, to be precise.

Pocket money

Laundry was deeply frustrating for my mother. She would hang clean clothes out on the line, and within five minutes they would be covered with greasy black smuts from the phurnacite. Collars, cuffs, sleeves…black, oily spots from top to bottom. It drove her, in common with all the other women in Mount and Abercwmboi, absolutely round the bend. But there was nothing to be done about it, try though they might. And try many of them did: letters, petitions, action groups…all to no avail.

The phurnacite plant that nestled on the valley floor within spitting distance of Mount Comprehensive had started out in life in 1939. Powell Dyffryn Limited had set it up to make briquettes out of the waste seam coal that was too small to use in any other way - or at least too small to sell profitably, no doubt. Most of the smoke was removed from these briquettes using a heating process of some kind I'll never understand, and at the height of its operation it produced a million tons of briquettes a year. That's one hell of a lot of coal products.

When I was a teenager I always thought 'briquette' a rather exotic word for this thing that caused so much mayhem around us. Dead blackened trees lined the valley slopes like something from a post-apocalyptic nightmare. Most of the briquettes were destined for England, which didn't help. *"That's right! Dump all your bloody crap on us before you burn your smokeless sodding fuel in your English sodding fireplace! Go on, ya bastards!"*

So, as I say, laundry was a big thing for my mother. Clean laundry, that is. She'd hang sheets on the line then go out an hour later to turn them, top to bottom, bottom to top, so they'd dry evenly. She taught me how to peg things out properly: pants the right way up, shirts the wrong. You never hang anything in a way that the peg marks show afterwards – on shoulders, for instance - and you use as few pegs as possible in case it starts 'picking with rain' and you have to fly out to get the whole lot in before it turns to cats and dogs. Or hail. We saw a lot of hail in Mount, some of it like golf balls. Mostly when there was washing on the line.

But...dirty laundry, now that was something else. That was something you should never hang out in public.

"Susan, you haven't asked me for money for sanitary things for ages." It is 1972. January. I haven't had a period for 4 months.

The words strike abject terror in my heart, but still I manage to reply faster than you can say 'pregnant'.

"I've been buying my own."

"What with?"

She's folding freshly-laundered bedding in the kitchen. I busy myself with my school books next door in the sitting-room, packing my satchel for the next day and avoiding eye contact.

"My pocket money." My voice comes out surly. It's not what I'd planned.

"Why? You don't get that much." She snaps the creases out of a pillow case. *Crack!*

"It's enough." I feel my face turning pink. I've always despised lying, but I'm becoming very adept at it – not least of all to myself. She folds a sheet ready for ironing, throwing it in the basket and picking up another pillow case. *Crack!*

"Well, you don't need to. You shouldn't have to pay for those things yourself. Ask me next time."

"OK!"

She's not satisfied. "So when do you think that'll be?" *Crack!*

"I don't know! A couple of weeks? Do you want me to look in my diary, or what?" Please don't! *Please.*

"No, that's fine. But just ask - alright?" She picks up the basket full of ironing. Why would you iron bedding! To my fifteen-year-old brain that just doesn't compute.

"Yes, alright." *Don't go on,* I'm thinking. I don't say it.

A month later she arranges an appointment at the doctor's.

I am lying on the couch in Dr. Lewis's surgery. My mother's sitting at his desk as he examines me, my tummy standing proud and firm above my ribs. My heart races, his hands pressing firmly, first one side then the other. Now he is pushing just above my pelvis. I know now of course that he was trying to size the baby to estimate my dates.

"Well, you're right, Mrs Jenkins. She's certainly pregnant. I'd say about five months." His hands are still gauging. I stare at the ceiling, trying to pretend this isn't happening to me. But it is. There's no escaping it now. He's the expert, and he has spoken. Nothing I say can make this go away. And nothing I do can deny there's a very real baby inside me, growing by the day.

Now he speaks to me: "Have you felt anything moving down here, Susan?" He's still prodding, my bump moving around under his hands.

"No," I lie. Again. He presses more firmly.

"Nothing like wind?"

"No, nothing." I can't bring myself to say the words, even though the game is clearly up. *Of course* I've felt movement. Every day I'm aware of this life growing inside me. Every day I'm terrified – absolutely terrified – what my mother will say when she finds out.

His face shows the concern of a doctor worried there might be some complication beyond a five-month-pregnant under-age mother. A moment later his face relaxes.

"Well, I can feel something go on there, so I'm sure it's all going fine. Just button yourself up and pop your shoes on, will you Susan."

Sitting himself down in the chair opposite my mother he asks her, "Have you thought about what you'll do at all, Mrs Jenkins?"

I put my shoes on and sit on the examination couch. I couldn't be further away from my mother right now if I was on a different planet. In one sense I am, I suppose.

"Yes. She's going to her sister's in Devon until the baby's born." He stops making notes and looks up at her. "Then it'll be adopted."

The words hit me like a whip across the face. The shock is something physical. Not only do they *know*, but my parents have called my sister in Plymouth, who I adore and trust, with I shared a bedroom with for years before she moved away and got married, and they've actually *carved up* my future without so much as a by-your-leave! I feel my chest will burst. Or is it my heart?

"Right. That's good." He returns to complete his notes. He can close the case on this one, now then.

"And how will you..."

"Everything's been arranged already," she cuts in. I can't believe what I'm hearing.

"And what about the school? Have you thought about..." He doesn't get the chance to finish his sentence.

"We're telling them she's gone away with nervous exhaustion."

We're telling them! Not *me!* I'm not involved in this for one minute! But why should I be? I'm only the person *carrying* this baby – only the one who'll put her life on the line giving birth...only the one who'll nurse it, and feed it, and bath it, and change it! Or maybe not. Maybe I won't even get to see it. Will I? Will I even know if it's a boy or a girl before they take it away? *Will* I?

My mother – this baby's grandmother - continues, 'She's supposed to be doing her O Levels doctor, and she's been working very hard…" *I haven't!* "…so that makes sense anyway."

Nothing makes sense! Not one word of this makes sense. This is *my* body, *my* life - what the hell do they think they're doing? What right do they think they've…..

"Well, that all sounds fine, then." He smiles in my direction as though they've just done me an enormous favour – as if I should be grateful I'm being 'looked after'. "Right – well there's nothing else, is there?" He looks over to my mother again.

"No, that's all thank you. I'm glad that's sorted."

"You must be, yes. Well, good luck, Mrs Jenkins."

"Thank you, doctor." And with that she is standing up.

"Susan," he says gently as he gets to his feet. For a moment I think he's about to ask me what I want, what this baby's mother wants in all of this. But he probably knows as well as I do that whatever I may want is irrelevant. I'm not the one who's going to be making any decisions here. "Look after yourself," he says. "And see you in a few months when this is all over."

I slide down off the couch, not feeling my feet touch the ground.

"Thank you," seems to be coming out of my mouth.

Our family doctor opens the door for us, and then we're out of his surgery, passing through the waiting room with my mother saying hallo brightly to someone who's arrived while we've been in there. No doubt she's praying nothing will have been overheard. Dirty linen should never be aired in public.

I recall very little of the next few days: nothing about the walk home from the doctor's that night, nothing about packing and leaving, and not a thing about the two hundred mile journey to Plymouth in a borrowed car with my father at the wheel.

What I do remember is lying on the sofa that evening after the doctor's, watching TV. I have no recollection what was on, but I remember the feeling as if it was yesterday – no, today; a moment ago. Because it's the only time I can ever remember lying with my head on my mother's lap, curled up under a blanket, with her hand tenderly stroking my hair, her fingers slowly running along my long, thick auburn locks as if every single strand was a precious gift. Apart from the time I spent at what was to become her death bed as she lay there in a coma after a massive stroke, holding her hand and stroking her cheek and telling her that I loved her, there was no other moment in my entire life when I felt so close to my mother.

Plymouth

In the decades after the war, lots of valleys folk migrated to the clean, fresh air of Plymouth, and it's easy to see why with that fabulous view over to the stunning Cornish coast, the historic Hoe. ('The whore' as my father pronounced it, "I'm going down on the whore for a while," causing much mirth on family holidays.) Then there were coastal resorts galore and the vast beautiful moorland named after the glorious River Dart. Here you could hang out your washing without fear; here you could get appointments to see doctors without queuing for half an hour in the cold and damp alongside men choking with emphysema, spewing their lungs out gobbing phlegm (if they could finally get it up) at your feet.

My fifteen-year-old fondness for what I saw as a utopian modern coastal city back then, though, was tinged with fear. I was there for a specific reason, and that reason bore no thinking about. So best not to, and it was my sister's job to make sure I didn't; by and large she made a great success of it.

Anne had been my second mother in Mount. Now she was to be my first here in sunny Devon. Herself only a young woman not long married, she'd had visions of a carefree life in Plymouth with her new teacher-husband. She'd left the valleys behind, with all that entailed. Misery and despair had been her constant companions back in Mount; here she could breathe, opening her heart to the possibility of a new kind of existence. Here she had started afresh, made a home – a safe one – and build a family that would be wanted, loved and cherished.

Then I came along. Again. Fifteen, pregnant and vulnerable. To add insult to injury, I was domestically totally useless: I couldn't boil an egg (OK, perfect egg boiling's not easy, but nor could I make anything more than a sandwich, and that was hit and miss); I'd never ironed, I didn't even really know how to wash dishes or use a washing machine. All these had just happened around me back home. So Anne taught me all these life skills and much, much more. She taught me that people can survive even the most traumatic events – if they're loved and supported. But that was tricky, I'd learn, because the giving and receiving of love I realise now has to start by loving oneself. Being fifteen and pregnant I didn't really even like myself very much, and I couldn't see why anyone should. All the 'love' I'd gone out and found had been procured through sex. So I certainly didn't understand loving oneself, much less so loving anyone else - not really. My mother had always thoroughly rejected the notion of loving oneself. To her, 'loving oneself' was all about ego: "I don't love myself, thank god. I'll never be one of those people who loves themselves." And then she'd reel off a list of people she considered *did* love themselves, followed by a catalogue their other flaws, all equally heinous. Bless her, she never did get her head around that self-acceptance/self-forgiveness thing. Maybe that helps explain why she struggled to show love for others - or struggled to feel love, even.

Nonetheless Anne welcomed me into her home with tenderness, love and compassion. This was no small thing. Even in the seventies in Plymouth, my situation would have been an embarrassment. Unmarried mothers were still stigmatised. 'Slut,' I'd have been, or 'tart'. Yet astonishingly I never experienced a shred of hostility or contempt – not from anyone in those months I spent in the care of my big sister. That was at least partly down to the tender arm of my siblings, who wrapped a protective cocoon around me as a mother-to-be. And maybe it's also that difference between the general and the specific: I was treated with nothing but kindness, despite the general attitude of disgust directed towards girls in 'my situation'. There were 'teenage mothers' but then there was 'me'. In the general we were cheap, with loose morals and lacking any sense of responsibility – the architects of our own demise. And yet on a personal level I was viewed as an unfortunate victim, the unlucky fish who got caught in an ocean of equally vulnerable youngsters. It was the same later with English university friends of mine coming home to Wales and, after the initial surprise that we had running water and didn't all live in caves, being surprised at the warm welcome. It ran completely counter to the infamous hostility of the Welsh for the English.

"But you hate the English! We all know that."

"Yes, we hate 'The English'. That doesn't mean we hate English *people* – not on an individual basis. We don't hate *you*, Rosie!"

You had to understand politics to get that. Rosie was my best friend at university. She was reading Politics. She should have got it. She came from a nice English suburb near Barnet. Barnet was the VD capital of the world at the time. Rosie didn't have VD. There was the general, and there was the specific.

So I was welcomed in Plymouth – by Anne's friends, her neighbours, and her friends' and neighbours' families. But we agreed to tell them I was sixteen. Being under-aged as well as unmarried was a tad too much even for the 'liberal' classes of Plymouth in 1972.

I have lots of fond memories of that time in Devon, in amongst the traumatic ones. Tourism in Devon was flourishing in the sixties and seventies. The country was enjoying an economic boom, with living standards rising rapidly. The car industry and related engineering in the South East and the Midlands, iron, steel and coal in the Welsh Valleys and the North of England, all provided good incomes that could run to a couple of weeks' holiday during 'Miners Fortnight' – the last two weeks of August, just before the schools went back. Most holidays back then were still taken in The UK, with Majorca and the Costa del Sol just starting to emerge as destinations for the more adventurous. So the tourist hub of Devon and Cornwall – *The British Riviera* – was a significant beneficiary of this major leap forward in British economic development. Bed-and-breakfasts flourished and caravan parks sprung up all over the place. Our own family holidays had begun to concentrate on visiting Anne and Jeff in their new home now that Jeff was establishing his career in Plymouth as a teacher. We were becoming very familiar with the popular and indeed the less well-known beauties of the South-West.

This time, however, I found myself there with an altogether different purpose and for a much longer time. This time I was there to get me through to the end of my pregnancy, to go through the whole birthing process, and then have my child taken by the adoption authorities. Social Services would take charge of me. While the rest of my year was sitting the O-Level Physics exam, I'd be undergoing a very different kind of test – one of surviving childbirth almost entirely single-handed at the age of fifteen. But that was to be a good four months off yet.

As I say, at home I'd never really paid much attention at all to the practicalities of running a home. Despite the suffragette movement, women's lib and the advances of feminism, men's tripling of their contribution to domestic chores from one per cent to three per cent still left the bulk of such responsibilities firmly with the section of the population with a womb. Somehow though I'd managed to side-step all such responsibility thus far. Oh, I'd mow the lawn now and then if my father asked, and I'd wipe the occasional dish; I'd been known to run out and help my mother gather in the laundry if it suddenly started to bucket down, and of course I'd pop to the grocer's with a list or help unpack it all if Ford's delivered for us. But cook? Iron, or wash up? Put a duster around, or clean up after myself? Why on earth would I want to do something like that? I was a theoretical product of women's emancipation – not realising at the time, of course, that my attitude therefore left the other women around me to do all the hard work so this little princess could busy herself with intellectual pursuits like…oh yes, shagging the boys instead of doing the dishes.

At Anne's it was different. At Anne's I was expected to play my part in helping out with light household chores – a suitably gentle easing in for baby sister with baby on board. Anne taught me to scrape carrots, peel potatoes, prepare celery *properly* without the stringy bits left dangling. Jeff taught me how to make creamy, butter-enriched mash with no lumpy bits. I learned how to iron shirts in the optimal order, thereby avoiding creasing sections already ironed, and eradication of silverfish from a pantry was a skill I hadn't even realised I lacked until I moved to the South-West. We grew vegetables and fruit, made crumbles and pies; I even mastered gravy-making, albeit a skill which slipped from memory faster than you could say, "Bisto!" We made beds with 'hospital corners' and I helped clean the car inside and out with proper chamois leathers and an acquired professionalism. I learned to shop on a strict budget - my parents sent none of my Child Benefit nor indeed any other financial support for my keep while I was living with Anne and Jeff – a skill much valued when I found myself at university. In short, I learned a whole load of life skills every fifteen-year-old should have, and for that I'm truly grateful. So I found myself a fully functioning part of Anne's family, with Plymouth increasingly feeling like home.

Life in Plymouth was not all work and no play, though. Surrounded by stunning coastal scenery within a very short drive from their home, this young married couple liked to make the most of their leisure time when life allowed. Visits to the National Trust's beautiful Bovisand were frequent and once I'd got over the embarrassment of my developing bulge, we even went swimming in a breath-takingly crisp English Channel. Picking our way down to some of the Cornish beaches could be precarious and the climb back up exhausting, but the golden sands and rock pools took me back to the trips we'd made as a larger family to Porthcawl and Barry Island when I'd been young and they'd been in their teens.

With no family car to our name back then in Wales, it had been long nauseous bus trips, all salmon and cucumber sandwiches and a bag to vomit in as we wound our way down the valley. I never travelled well as a child. Or the Chapel Outing to Barry, where it always seemed God was thinking about us and had kept a special bit of hailstone back just for the Baptists. Huddling under the stone arcade running alongside the beach we managed to protect ourselves from the lashing rain, but nothing could keep the biting wind from whipping around our plastic macs, bare legs in short white sock goose-bumped like pebbledash and shivering with cold, plastic hats tied on tight. Most times the rain stopped at some point and we'd get to sit on the sea wall munching through wagon wheels. My mother's memory was of an August that was always long and hot – "proper summers, like they're meant to be." Hmm. Funny that. Doesn't tally with mine.

Playgroup

Anne worked as a playgroup leader for pre-school children in the early seventies, and while I lived with her I leapt at the chance to go along as another pair of hands. I'd always loved children, and as a youngster I'd happily walked neighbours' babies around and around the block trying to get them to sleep. My career ambition in my teens had been to train as a Maths teacher – but that was in the days before I discovered Economics and Politics as disciplines.

The under-fives in Plympton Playgroup were very sweet. I hadn't realised quite how much assistance would be needed in the tying up of shoe laces (this was in the pre-velcro days) and putting back on of trousers after a visit to the toilet. Nor had I realised the endless opportunities for misinterpreting what to a fifteen-year-old seemed screamingly obvious.

"Why is your tummy so big?" asked a four-year-old boy.

"My tummy? Oh, there's a baby in there," I replied, all smiles and ready to explain but not sure just how much detail I was expected to provide for such a tiny person.

William (four) looked at my bump then stared me straight in the face with an expression of absolute horror before running off to one of my sister's assistants. Minutes later, Anne came over to clear the matter up.

"William thinks you eat babies," she laughed.

"Oh my god! Do you want me to explain?"

"No, it's alright. Janet's filling him in on the finer details of where babies grow. He probably won't believe her!"

Later, as we cleared up after milk and biscuits, little Sarah who'd taken a shine to me came up and reassured me, "William said you eat babies, but I don't believe him. I told him you just eat too much ice cream. My mummy told me that makes you fat."

I was tempted to send her in Janet's direction too, but found myself lying, "I think your mum's right, Sarah. Mums know a lot of things, you know." With the wide-eyed innocence I guess I too had once had, she replied, "My mum knows everything." If only.

That evening Anne and I went to the cinema in town just up from Union Street, the red light area in this dockland city. As we stood on the street corner licking our ice creams, reading the notice of films to come, both of us young women with almost waist-length brunette hair and my bump invisible from behind, two young men approached us.

"Scuse girls, fancy a drink?"

We turned. I expanded instantly in front of their eyes, and they were gone before we could draw breath, leaving us sisters chuckling at the smoke from their military heels.

Night-time was the most difficult during those months. No matter how tired I was – even if I'd drifted off in the car on a return journey from a day out, or on the sofa in front of the TV – getting to sleep was always a struggle. Lying in bed with nothing to distract me, I'd become increasingly aware of every movement, every squirm, every wriggle, every turn as this baby adjusted from this position to that. Or hiccoughs. I hadn't realised then that babies in the womb could have hiccoughs, swallowing some of the amniotic fluid and setting off a series of spasms. I'd feel a foot move from my right side to my left, or a whole body shift from head pressing into my stomach to a position in readiness for engagement and birth - and heartburn like I've never known since, with no medication I could take to alleviate it.

Night-time was hard. It was the time when thoughts crowded in, competing with one another to see which might keep me awake the longest tonight, which might cause me most grief. At times I'd slip out of bed and stand at the window with its vista of the traffic weaving up and down the final stretch of the A38 as it fed down the valley, then onto Marsh Mills roundabout and veering off up Crown Hill towards the Moors and Cornwall, or down to the left along the Embankment running beside the Plym and into the centre of town. I'd gaze out over the rooftops, away into the twinkling distance of headlights all heading somewhere. Where? What was their destination?

Maybe I could gather a few things in a bag, step silently out into the night air, walk the half-mile down to that interchange of roads, and raise my thumb. Maybe I could take my road untravelled, a road to somewhere I could hold onto my child - a road to anywhere but that room where they'd take my child from me. Anywhere.

Standing there, elbows on the windowsill gazing out down to the A38, with Devon then Cornwall then the rest of the world beyond...would it *really* matter to anyone at all if I disappeared from here? Would *anyone's* life be less fulfilled if I was gone? Oh, for a while, yes. That's always the case. But afterwards?

I found it hard to convince myself there'd be much damage to anyone's welfare if I left. Now. And went god knows where. The cars sped on, their rear lights disappearing into the blue-black of the world beyond the one I knew.

As for me, if I ran I'd still have my baby; it would have me. And what was that worth? For me it was worth the world to be able to hold onto this baby now. I'd give anything to hold onto this child. But the baby? What did I possibly have to offer the baby? Myself. That's all. That was it. Me. Nothing else. And this fifteen-year-old from Mount really didn't amount to very much at all.

What can I give him? Words flow into my head. Mrs Brace had taught us to sing them, in the school choir. Christina Rossetti. My favourite Christmas Carol; Harold Darke. What can I give him, poor as I am? If I were a shepherd, I would bring a lamb. If I were a wise man, I would do my part. Yet, what I can, I give him – give my heart. That's all I can do, my love. All I can give you is my heart. I stand there stroking my bump. Give my heart – that's all I can do, baby. Not enough. Clearly not enough. I'd been told repeatedly it was best for me, best for baby. Adoption. A nice new shiny family, with a nice big shiny house and a nice secure job with a good fat pension, no doubt. Even a brother. The baby was going to have a brother! Certainly not something I could give. In fact, not one of these was something I could give.

What was I even thinking of? I had absolutely nothing to give this baby. Nothing! How could I be so selfish? No, it was true – it was best for all concerned that this baby was going for adoption, hate it though I might. I'd just have to get used to it.

An elbow dug me in the ribs. It seemed there was someone could read my thoughts.

A Nice Day Out

It was great to be able to enjoy such wonderful countryside while I was living down in Devon. The weekend I was due to give birth we climbed the moor beside Burrator Reservoir. I'm not sure whose bright idea that was, looking back. Jeff's, I think, and he was a PE teacher, so that would explain it. And days before I was about to drop we all went for a drive to the coast.

Peter too had moved down to Plymouth by now, having exhausted the possibilities of spreading his wings while still living in Mount. It was great to have him there too, and the four of us did a lot together. Anne frequently fed him, for a start, and Peter and Jeff reminisced about crazy moments in school – the humour of schoolboys, leaving us dying with laughter when it came to Simon and his...no, I can't tell that one.

That drive to the coast with me forty weeks pregnant was in Peter's Morris Minor. Lets's just say I remember it well!

Black and smelling of ancient leather, Peter's car was a relic of the fifties, and I recognised it was something special even though it rattled the bones to distraction and the baby from sleep.

We head out for the day to Noss Mayo, a beautiful village on a tidal creek in the Yealm Estuary some ten miles out of Plymouth. A ten-minute walk from the sea, we sit awhile on the quay and watch the boats. The walk up and along the cliffs is good exercise for me, but we have to take it in stages. I must be carrying a couple of stone by now, with baby and water combined. The sandwiches Anne made taste all that much better in the sea air of Mothecombe beach. By evening we're more than ready for supper in The Ship Inn. Then I'm even more ready for bed. It's nine by the time we set off in the Morris. I'm in the back with Anne, drifting off to sleep.

Someone decides we should take a different route home, through the country lanes instead of the main roads – it will be shorter (a bit) and would be prettier (a lot) if only it was light. The further we get from civilisation, the more beautiful it would have become. And remote. And when the car begins to make odd little noises, we think little of it at first.

"It's OK," Pete reassures. "It does that." He's right. It does it again. Then again.

"Peter?" I hear Anne ask.

"Yes?"

"Why does it do that?" There's a slight edge to her voice.

"It's OK. We're just a bit low on petrol."

We roll on, the splutters becoming more frequent. "Peter…"

"Yeah?" He looks at Anne in the mirror, willing her not to ask. She does. "*How* short on petrol?"

We're still miles from home – indeed, miles from anywhere, now. It's a Sunday evening, approaching nightfall, and no traffic whatsoever on the road apart from us.

"It's OK. It'll be fine."

It isn't. Spluttering furiously now, then sounding like it's going to choke, Morris finally shakes us half to death as we grind to a halt.

"Ah." Silence. "OK." Peter clearly has a plan.

"OK what?"

"OK, we need to think."

"Yes, we do!"

We have no food, no water, no kettle, clean towels or anything else you need for a birth. These are the days before mobile phones; the days when petrol stations close by five on a Sunday if they open at all; the days before Sunday opening hours and supermarkets with petrol forecourts. We all realise there may actually be no way of getting petrol until tomorrow morning, and I'm evidently not up to walking anywhere.

This was promising to be quite a night.

"Right," says Jeff.

"Right what?" asks Anne, the guardian of her baby sister and the baby she's carrying – but for god knows how much longer. Or shorter. I feel a Braxton-Hicks contraction kick in, hoping it is indeed Braxton-Hicks instead of the real thing. "Oooh!"

Anne is concerned, but trying hard to hide it. "You're OK. It's just a practice one. Don't worry."

"Is she OK?" Jeff asks.

"She's fine."

I'm really not at all sure I am. That was a big one, and it hurt. A lot. A lot! I change position. This is like the worst attack of period pains I've ever had in my life! Maybe if I pretend it's not happening it'll go away. Owww! Bugger – that didn't work, did it!

"Peter's right. We need to think," Jeff adds.

Anne takes my hand. "It'll be fine. We'll be OK. Don't worry. Why don't you get out and walk about a bit?"

So we do, while the boys devise a plan out of earshot.

"Right," Peter says again, getting out of the car.

"Will you stop saying 'Right'!" Anne has too many scenarios running through her head, and not one of them is filling her with joy and rapture.

"No, I mean we've got a plan."

"Which is?"

So Peter and Jeff walk off down the road, petrol can in hand. (Peter is, we learn later, quite used to this: he does it again on the way to Granny's funeral, with me and my mother in the car – we never make the service. It becomes a bit of a pattern for Mother and me, this not making funerals thing.)

Anne and I watch as the two young men disappear over the top of the hill. It is, we reckon, a nine-mile round walk home to get Jeff's car and drive back via a garage; or maybe they'll use a tube to suck out some petrol from his tank. Either way, it's going to be a long wait. It's clear I have no option but to *not* give birth within the next few hours. OK, that was that sorted.

We play *I Spy* while it's still light – it'll be pretty boring in an hour or so. "I spy with my little eye something beginning with S."

"Star."

"Yep. But a different one this time. That one over there."

"That's a planet."

"How do you know?"

"I just do."

"We'll ask Jeff when he gets back."

Jeff likes his stars. He has one named after him now. There's a certificate on his wall telling him what number star is called Jeff Morgan. Anne has one too. 'Anne Morgan,' it is.

"What time is it?"

"Nearly half past nine."

We play noughts and crosses with pencil and paper we find in the dashboard, but the pencil snaps and there's no sharpener. So we listen to the radio for a while, but Anne's worried the battery will run down, and Jeff may not have jump leads. It's amazing how many ways you can entertain yourself inventing things to worry about in a car in a West Country lane with a terminally pregnant fifteen-year-old beside you.

Anne is praying they'll be back before the first contractions. I'm hoping they make it before the mad axeman does. Not that there's really a mad axeman, but you never know. I have a very active imagination at the age of fifteen-going-on-sixteen and pregnant.

Owls hoot close by – two of them, call and response, call and response. It reminds me of films like Dracula. The bats that were here, swooping and diving, have long since disappeared, thank god. It's getting cold. My big sister puts her arm around me to keep me warm. I don't know if she realises how much I need that right now, but I suspect she does.

"Oooohh!!" I jump with this one. It's stronger than anything I've felt so far.

"Just breathe. You're fine. In…..out, slowly. Well done. Again. In…." It passes. "OK. I name an animal beginning with A, then you do B, and so on. Alligator."

"Bear."

"Crocodile."

*   *   *   *

"What time is it?"

"Ten past twelve."

It's getting really cold now, despite being June. The sky is clear, laser-bright stars burning through the sky's velvet drape.

I drift in and out of sleep. The sea air and impending motherhood have worn me out. Anne stays on guard. I dream of playing at home on the floor in Hughes Street with Peter's Scalextric. He's put the track together and we're just about to start our first race. The two of us sprawled out on the floor, I look at his face, his eyes behind his Joe 90 glasses focused intently on the egg-timer that will start our race. "Three, two, one, go!" But the cars won't start. He's forgotten to put petrol in. Again!

An hour later we see headlights in the distance. They flash as they approach.

"That'll be them," says Anne, sighing with relief. "At last."

"That'll be the mad axeman," I think. It's not. This time Big Sister really does know best.

Shopping

When a baby's on the way there are certain routines you have to go through which to your standard mother – one who'll go on to keep her child – are unambiguously thrilling. One such event is buying what's known as the 'layette': a crib, soft blankets, nappies, maybe a stuffed rabbit. None of this, of course, is necessary in my case. There will be no choosing of colours for the nursery walls, no stencils of Jemima Puddleduck with a lightshade to match. I'll be hanging no mobile above a cot in the corner of the room designed to be most conducive to sleep-filled nights and harmonious days.

One thing, however, does need to be bought: the baby's first outfits – babygrows in lemon and pastel green. It doesn't even occur to me that pink or blue might be starting a life-long engendering process – not at the age of fifteen. And in any case not only do I not know the baby's sex of course, but the eight days we'll have together will be as the blinking of an eye in the life long period of separation in which some other mother will do the nurturing and socialisation. From Day 9 it will be a complete stranger who will shape the adult my child will become. Spending that first eight days in a socially-prescribed colour would count for nothing in this baby's life.

At the age of fifteen I cannot begin to imagine how important that first long week will become for me in the bonding process, nor the scars it will leave when my baby's wrenched from my arms, denied this mother's breast.

Mothercare wasn't a shop I was familiar with as a teenager. Very unsurprising really. The chain itself was nascent and slowly growing, and there was no-one in my family who had young children; nor did any family friends. This store opened a whole tantalising treasure trove for me, opening too a channel I couldn't have anticipated: walking in through those doors into an emporium of mother–and–baby goods seemed to kick–start something hormonal, something emotional from absolutely nowhere. Physically handling those delicate tiny new-born garments brought it right home that this fast-growing bump was indeed a small person. My son or daughter. This was another human being inside me, not just something causing me the inconvenience of constant visits to the doctor, the midwife, Social Services; the trauma of leaving home, missing my exams, probably repeating a year – if, that was, I even decided to continue with my schooling at all. No – developing inside me were the arms to go into these tiny sleeves, the feet that would fit tenderly and with great care into the bottom of this minute babygrow. Handling these garments had the effect of concretising this child of mine in a way that none of the books, the anti-natal examinations, the endless blood tests and the urine samples had come close to. The texture of the fabrics, all having been chosen for their softness next to that delicate new born skin; the sheer scale of these clothes… that bonnet with its frill around the edge and the exquisitely embroidered rim….the colours themselves all neutral and calming. Dungarees with a simple tractor on the front, poppers for changing nappies with ease. Everything had been designed with baby's comfort in mind.

My fingers run along the rack of white frocks, red roses dotted around the hem – each one a drop of blood I would shed too soon, touching the skirts of this child I will carry a very short while longer. I take a miniscule sock in my hand, its cuff turned back with a pink bow. Another is blue.

"I don't think we need socks. They're not on the list." Anne holds in her hand the piece of paper Miss Featherstone helpfully provided us with. The list from my social worker is short. She doesn't want us buying unnecessary items. No nappies – they will be provided by the hospital in the first instance and then by the stranger. No outdoor clothing – we won't be stepping out into the Devon air, negotiating shop doors, exploring local parks. In fact we won't be allowed beyond the ward for the whole time we're together. The tall white walls will be the boundary of our world, our life together, forever. I put the socks back on the shelf alongside all those other superfluous items. My bag is almost empty as we leave the store, and yet I have every single item I will ever need for my child.

We should not, the list implies, be going to any unnecessary expense. No, of course not: the new mother will want to start from scratch. She might even discard everything I have in this basket. It suddenly crosses my mind that she's probably bought everything already. It occurs to me as we approach the till that any one of the women I've seen in here who isn't visibly pregnant could happen to be the woman who will take my baby. I scan their faces in alarm. Could she actually be in here now, buying things for my child just as I am? That woman there, trying out that pram, is that her? Could that be her? I feel panic starting to rise. I have to get out of the shop. I drop the bag on the counter and hurry towards the door, empty-handed.

"Are you alright, Susan?" Anne is suddenly alarmed as I turn.

"Yes. I…I just need…"

"Do you want a chair?"

"No, I…"

"Some water?" She's following me to the door, past the racks of babygrows.

"No. I just need to get out of here." And I can't explain. I can never explain. Because it makes no difference who'll be taking my baby; 'taken' is what my child will be.

And then I need – I want – to buy something I can leave with him or her forever. But what do you leave with a child so that maybe – just maybe – one day they'll look at it and think, "Yes, she did love me"?

There will be no Christmas presents, no gift on a birthday. There will be nothing for passing exams, achievements in sport, a driving test, Grade One in Guitar… an eighteenth birthday, coming of age. Not one of them will see the exchange of gifts. So what to give on parting that the child will one day know that it was loved? A piece of jewellery, we decided. Something to last, a keepsake that will have been chosen with care; something that will be there for as long as this child might want something of me in his or her life.

Having returned to the store and completed the transaction, we carry our Mothercare bag through Plymouth City Centre, stopping at every jeweller's in our attempt to find something I can afford with the very little money I have. My few rather feeble suggestions are met with a gentle evasive tactic on the part of my wise sister.

"Come on… let's just take a look down the road." I'm struggling to find anything half-respectable with the cash in my hand.

Finally we decide to go in and ask advice from a kindly-looking woman despite her chain's uniform of black and white. We explain we're looking for a birthing present, a keepsake, for a new baby and it must surely be clear which baby we're buying for.

"Of course. How lovely! When's it due?"

"About three weeks."

"How exciting." If only she knew.

We're presented with a range of goblets we could engrave (but to whom, from whom? Too many explanations required), photo frames we could fill (but would that be allowed? And what with, anyway?) and finally we fix on a bracelet – the most delicate, tiny bracelet for this child's wrist.

"But we don't know if it's a girl," I remark.

"Oh, parents buy these for either," the woman offers reassuringly. It must be sterling silver, Anne insists. It is. We pay for it, and it's tenderly placed in a presentation box and gift-wrapped.

"They're often given as Christmas presents," she tells us, imagining we're going to have a future life together, mother and child on this journey called life. It flashes through my mind that if there's to be a Christening, I won't be there. Nor for the many Christmases. Santa. Sleigh bells. Waiting to hear Rudolph on the roof. None of it. I feel sick again, and wait outside while Anne collects the box and receipt.

No, I won't be there. At least my bracelet might.

Waiting

They say women's lives are shaped by waiting. There's a poignant poem I heard in some distant past about waiting for the phone to ring, waiting for Mr Right, waiting for him to pop the question, waiting for the baby to arrive. Waiting for the baby to arrive. Waiting and waiting. Wanting and not wanting. Wanting to get this over and done with, to get back to Mount, to get on with 'real life', get on with being a teenager.

Rather naively it had never really occurred to me that anything could go seriously wrong during pregnancy. I suppose that as a child and then a young teenager back in the seventies, global events had relatively recently begun to appear on the television, so we knew very little about conditions across the world. I recall seeing dreadful images of starving children in the 1960s Biafran famine, all the more shocking because for the first time we were seeing actual moving images of real children dying in front of our eyes. But this was a rare and early glimpse of the terrible fate that was befalling others across the globe. Maternal, infant and pre-natal mortality wasn't something I was familiar with. Even my Geography lessons had focused on Wales, on map symbols, on the height of the *Tumpy* across the valley. There was a whole world out there about which I knew practically nothing, and the potential hazards of pregnancy and childbirth had passed me by completely, hadn't even crossed my mind up to that point.

Around the time I'm eight months pregnant I develop a backache. Nothing debilitating, but I a pain on my right side in the middle of my back as I sit down and stand back up again. That's hardly surprising: I'm carrying a good-sized baby by all accounts, and that's bound to take its toll. For several days I try to ignore it (fast becoming a favourite strategy of mine), convincing myself it will go away. It doesn't. In fact it becomes pretty excruciating, to the point that I can barely get out of a chair without breaking into a sweat. Finally I tell Anne and she does the responsible thing of making an appointment at the doctor's first thing the following morning. Urine tests are promptly despatched and I'm told to rest and take it easy. I cannot, of course, take anything for the pain, which by now is reducing me to tears.

Imagine our surprise when later that day our rather lovely female family doctor appears at the front door with powerful antibiotics in hand, insisting I take a double dose immediately and then strictly every six hours. If there's no improvement within twenty-four hours or any suggestion of things getting worse, I'm to get to A and E straight away. It seems I have a severe kidney infection and the baby's life could be in danger. In fact, had I not seen the doctor that day, the consequences might well have been very grave indeed.

At that moment it hits me like a mallet that this bump, this growing baby, is an independent but also entirely dependent little person in its own right, and that my responsibility to this other human being here is absolute. That responsibility weighs on me enormously. What was I doing here, in terms of my every action affecting so directly one whole person with an independent life ahead of them? Even one day's delay might have…. In not wanting to make a fuss about my*self*, I'm also not been a good advocate for this most vulnerable of people here, in my womb. I've put this child's life at risk because I didn't want to 'bother' anyone. I've brought enough trouble and concern to everyone already; the last thing I want is to add to the bother I've already caused. And yet inadvertently I've almost…I've nearly…

It doesn't bear thinking about.

It's clearly time for me to wake up to the fact that while I might not want to make any demands on my *own* behalf, I absolutely must make them on behalf of this baby. What *I* want is now of secondary importance. This baby's welfare has to come first. It has to come before everything else from this moment on.

I sit in Anne's garden. It's May turning June, Spring into Summer, and today Anne turns twenty-three. The sun beats down on their sheltered patio and I'm wishing we had a canopy or something, anything to shade us from this scorching Whitsun Devonian heat, but I want to stay in the sun. Heavy pregnancy makes everything hotter it

SUSAN J BEVAN

seems, and yet I sit and wait while Anne prepares a long, cool iced tea. What feels like a foot jerks up towards my ribs. This baby's been engaged for some time now, so movements have slowed right down to the occasional wriggle and an odd nudge.

Feet up to prevent my legs from swelling further, I turn the page in my birth and new-motherhood book, the second half of which is of no use whatsoever to me. Nonetheless I read bits of it, fascinated.

The first trip out can be a daunting time for any new mother, and it is no bad idea to have someone with you first time around. Even getting up the steps into the newsagent can be a challenge for the most able new mum! But don't worry – it will all be second nature in no time at all.

Still I'm behaving as if this isn't happening to me, remarkable as that might seem when I'm at this very late stage. I read the pages like an academic book. This might just as well be a revision guide for Biology for all I'm concerned, the emotional part of my brain being decidedly supressed much of the time.

"How're you doing?" Anne emerges cheerily with two tall glasses clinking with ice. Why shouldn't she? It's her birthday, after all! I'm lucky to be spending it with her; I've missed the last few, with her down here and us in Mount. Not so this time. Every cloud…

On the tray she's brought a piece of home-made banana cake to keep our energies up. She's all too aware of the need for healthy eating and a healthy lifestyle, having developed a heart condition herself as a child.

"I'm fine. Just looking at this forceps thing." She hands me my afternoon snack. "Thanks."

"Oh, you don't want to worry about all that. I'm sure you won't need them. And if you do," she adds hastily, "they'll be really gentle. You'll be fine." Sitting down beside me she adds, "Gosh, it's hot out here!"

"I wish I just knew…y'know…when."

"I'm sure everybody feels like that." She breaks off a piece of cake and pops it in her mouth. "It'll be soon enough, just you wait."

Waiting for the birth to start, waiting for the pain to end, waiting for the dawn to rise when I'm back in Mount, back in my own bed, in my own home, in my own life. Waiting.

I got a letter from Janice Bowen today. She says my Gran told her mother I was suffering from nervous tension because of the exams. Was that true? Whatever the reason I'm down in Plymouth, she's really sorry I'm not well and hopes I'll be better soon. What's it like down there? Somebody said Devon was really nice, with good beaches and things. Was I going swimming? Was the water freezing? Mark, an ex-boyfriend of mine, was asking about me, and she didn't know what she should tell him. Should she say I was suffering from nervous exhaustion? Or should she tell him to mind his own business? Carol was going out with Robert now, and Mr Thomas went crazy when he caught Lynda behind the bike sheds with Phil, but apart from that there wasn't anything going on in Mount. When did I think I'd be back? She had the Maths exam on Monday and she wished I was there because she came out feeling rubbish – it was impossible! There were loads of questions on things she's never seen before. Were there any fanciable blokes in Plymouth? If there were, could I send one up for her, because there was a serious shortage in Mount. Write soon, Suse!

I should write to Granny. But what can I say? What *can* I say to my Gran?

Time

During lunch on Sunday the fourth of June I begin to realise these contractions aren't Braxton Hicks. Mild panic begins to sweep through me and, not for the first time, I try to convince myself this isn't happening to me. I'm becoming pretty well-practised at this self-delusion business.

Having had no preparation whatsoever for this impending birth - no ante-natal classes, no support group for teen mothers-to-be as one might today - I am, frankly, terrified. To be fair Anne's done more than her best, giving me umpteen excellent books on pregnancy and birth. But I've barely been able to face them: every one of them seems to have a celebratory tone about becoming a mother; every one of them has chapters on bonding, on arriving home as a new mother, on managing excited visitors while building in enough rest as a new mum with a demanding if beautiful new addition to the family; every one of them makes me want to weep.

And as for the question of why there have been no ante-natal classes, I can only imagine now that no-one had wanted to frighten me. Less is more, as they say. Or maybe it was to save face, protecting me from discrimination.

Well, whatever the reason I'm going into this birthing business in one sense with my eyes firmly closed; in every other sense I can't take my mind's eye off images I've seen of a woman in labour. As clear as day I can see our sex education class from school. Fifteen year-olds watching *Helga*, a film following a woman all the way through from the very first stages of pregnancy up to baby's delivery - everything shown in full, graphic detail. And now all I can see is Helga laid out on her back, in absolute agony: the groaning, the blood, the sweat, the tears, and then finally what appeared to be an enormous rugby ball of a head emerging slowly and painstakingly from inside her, someone's fingers easing this woman open to help the baby finally through. It was horrific, and followed after a moment's respite by the shoulders and then quickly by the rest of the body as it almost catapulted out in one enormous bloody gooey slither, with what appeared to be a purple rope attached to its belly, the umbilical cord long and meaty.

All I can think is that all of this is inside me now, and all of it has to get out somehow. Somehow! I know precisely *how*, of course. I understand the *biology* of it as well as any new mother might. But my fifteen-year old imagination is in overdrive. The thought flashes through my mind that women still die in childbirth - even now in the 1970s women are still dying giving birth to their children. And although I have no idea what really lies ahead of me, what I do know is that it's going to be a trial, an epic journey like I don't even dare imagine.

One might have thought my earlier experiences months before of convincing myself I wasn't pregnant in the face of every shred of evidence screaming to the contrary, might have had some kind of impact on me...that I might actually speak to my sister straight away about my fear my time has come. At least this time, unlike the last, I have her beside me – loving, caring, supportive...ready to deal with anything I present.

But no! Yet again I try to ignore the imminent arrival of my baby, try to pretend this isn't really happening to me - not me. Not now. Ignore it and it'll go away.

Sitting in the toilet, I grip my stomach for dear life, "Please God, don't let this be happening to me. Please!" Futile. But still I sit, and grip, and sit some more.

"Susan, are you alright?" Anne knocks on the bathroom door.

Attentive as ever to my welfare, my sister is all too aware this could be the big day. My dates have never been very clear, but the baby is certainly, clearly, evidently due to be born any moment now. It's been in position for weeks, lying low beneath my ribs and just waiting for hormones to kick in.

"Yeah, I'm fine. Just going to the toilet."

Unbelievable! Why! Why? Why not just, "No, I think it's started, and I'm scared stiff."

But no. Not me. This child is about to arrive whether I say it or not. This event is completely beyond my control. Why pretend? Denial is only likely to make things more painful: stress is sure as hell not going to help my labour. But still I try to suppress the rising panic. Ignore it. It'll go away. But no. Birth's not like that.

By the end of the afternoon there's no alternative. Contractions ripping through my young body, I'm now convinced the baby's arrival is imminent. Period pains I'm used to; sometimes I miss school, and always I'm on medication, but this…this is something else. Finally I have to both admit to myself and confide in Anne that I'm in the first stage of labour. She calls her doctor's (now our doctor's) emergency number to ask if we ought to head off to hospital. Implausible though it seems to me, the description we give indicates that I'm still only in the very early stages of labour; they suggest we wait a few hours before heading in. I can't believe I'll have to endure hours more of this. How naive could I have been!

By seven o'clock I can wait no longer and the contractions are close enough for me to be admitted. Anne, herself only twenty-three and seriously under-prepared for the events which have been thrust upon her, must surely by now be keen to get some professionals involved in her young sister's care. So we calmly collect a few last-minute things, my toothbrush and slippers, my best lemon chiffon nightie especially bought for the occasion, and pop them in my waiting bag, packed weeks before. And then I leave my sister's house, the short-term home that has come to feel such a safe place to be, for the last time as a pregnant teenager. The next time I step over that threshold it will be with a baby in my arms, I believe.

Little do I know.

Freedom Fields

The car on this warm summer's evening seems to glide up to the hospital site with distressing lack of speed, every moment seeming an hour. Never the fastest of drivers, Jeff is particularly cautious with a labouring youngster on board. Anne, torn between excitement and anxiety, checks constantly that I'm alright. I assure her I definitely am.

I so definitely am not.

Originally built as Plymouth Workhouse in 1858, Freedom Fields Hospital was enlarged several times before becoming first Greenbank Infirmary in 1909 and then Plymouth City Hospital in the early thirties. Being a prominent target on top of a hill in a crucial naval city, it had been regularly bombed during the war.

Standing before me now, its tall grey stone walls filled me with horror. Gothic it isn't, but to me it might as well be. It smells of the unknown, of despair and especially fear attacking my senses as we heave open the tall glass doors. Corridors, cream with acid green woodwork. The grey metallic lift is large enough to take hospital beds, but its walls close in on me as the doors clank shut.

Claustrophobic at the best of times, the prospect of being caught in a failing lift at this precise moment and in these particular circumstances freezes me to the bone. I shiver. 'Freedom Fields' indeed.

Registration is straight-forward, if slow. Enemas follow – emptying the bowels is a routine part of preparation for childbirth, it seems – and then the horribly humiliating practice of shaving pubic hair. The ubiquitous blood pressure, internal examinations, external examinations, monitoring the baby's heartbeat - all carried out without as much as a word to me. My sister is my advocate. I am a minor - just

135

the vehicle for this baby. Not even the mother-to-be. Fifteen, and deemed next to useless in terms of providing any sensible information, and why should I need to know anything about the proceedings anyway? It would probably petrify me, with no good purpose.

Or, I wonder now, was there more to it than that? Some twenty years later I was to read other women's accounts of being young unmarried mothers, especially teens, in the sixties and seventies – the years in which women's liberation had suggested we could 'have it all' as it were, especially control over our own fertility. But of course the so-called liberation hadn't got as far as recognising the need to provide contraception to young vulnerable under-age women. As a result, many of us who were sexually active became a steady flow of valleys, and other, girls to nursing homes in Devon. Many weren't treated well. We must remember that these were disapproving times when it came to teenage sex. We were the personification of all that was wrong with the so-called permissive society, and for some it was imperative we were 'punished'. Maybe I'm being harsh. But my care as a teenage mother giving birth was far from ideal. So it was for many others.

At nine o'clock on Sunday evening visitors are required to leave the hospital. My sister heads home with her husband, and I feel totally and utterly alone. I have of course absolutely no idea whatsoever what's ahead of me. A final examination, a mug of Horlicks –the first time I ever taste it and the smell still takes me right back there to that ward - a crossword puzzle book we've packed to take my mind off the contractions (I wish!) and a nurse shows me where the bell is if I need help. And then my lights are turned out, other than a bedside reading lamp. I'm told to try to get some sleep - chance would be a fine thing – and then I'm left. Alone.

The silence and sense of isolation are disorientating. Is this really how a maternity ward is? It seems there's no-one else in the entire hospital but me. Maybe it's a busy night. Maybe they're hard-pressed in another area of the maternity section. Maybe I'm the only admission and the nurses have fallen asleep! Or maybe, as many unmarried mothers from my time have suggested (and some nurses too), there is indeed a culture of punishing us, of leaving us deliberately unattended, either to teach us a lesson in the charitable hope we'll take every precaution against finding ourselves in this situation again or, more darkly, in a belief that we are genuinely *bad*. Whatever the reason, I don't see a soul until well beyond sunrise the next morning.

I spend that night in half-trauma. I cry. A lot. I pray – Granny always said her prayers before going to sleep, and always thanked God for the gift of another day. As a child (what am I now, if not a child?) I often silently prayed he'd perform a miracle on her, curing that agonising disease of hers. He hadn't answered back then, her legs increasingly bowed, her back progressively stooped. I couldn't see why He should answer me now. I was far less deserving of His compassion.

In my fifteen-year-old brain I've already worked out this pain can only mean something is seriously wrong inside me. I know this is it: I'm going to die. I'm only sorry it will be in this room, alone - that I'll never have the chance to tell everyone how sorry I am I've brought this on everyone. But I know my fate, and I accept it. I even convince myself that death is all I deserve. I behaved irresponsibly – more than once; then I lied to my mother about being pregnant, and I lied to the social worker when I said I'd only once had sex; and then I lied to my sister about being OK the day before, when I was in agony. I'm obviously a compulsive liar on top of everything else, and there were plenty of other sins I must have committed if only I could think hard enough. But I can't think of anything, because all the time here it is, another contraction, another surge. And anyway, why should God save me? No, I'm going to die, and I deserve it.

The night drags on, my contractions rising and falling then rising further. I cry off and on into my pillow to muffle the sound, tears hot on my face in that stuffy side ward, trying to prepare for my death as best you can at fifteen, alone, between contractions. I pray and pray. I hope I'll end up in heaven, because the alternative isn't worth thinking about.

I suppose now that it must have been the changeover of shift that brought a nurse into my room.

"Right, sweetheart. Let's have a little look, shall we?" She even smiles. Sweat pours off me, mingled with tears.

"Gosh, you've done well, haven't you." It's the first time I can recall being spoken to in my own right since I walked in through the door.

"Really?"

"Yes, you're doing really well there. Let's just take your blood pressure, shall we?"

Another wave of searing pain. I'm well on my way through the first stage of labour. I have no idea what time it is, but around 7.30 my sister has the most extraordinary shot of period pains ever – with no associated period. She certainly has a sort of sixth sense – but maybe we all do? Either way, she's convinced they're sympathetic labour pains. So driving to school and passing close to Freedom Fields, Jeff calls in to see how I'm getting on.

Poor Jeff. When he briefly pops in around 8.30 I'm on gas-and-air, struggling towards the last stages of birthing this child. He isn't met with the calm, quiet and glorious event he might have anticipated but with a child messily struggling through the agonies of labouring a first baby, petrified and in a great deal of pain. The gas mask is practically pinned to my face at that stage and after a few encouraging remarks Jeff leaves pretty sharpish, face white as candlewax and with the legs of a drunk. He almost couldn't make it down the stairs.

Alison Jenkins is born at 9.30 on a Monday morning, the fifth of June – or so it was recorded. I can't say how much attention was given to the precise time, to the absolute minute, but I imagine it's as close as practically necessary in a hospital. It just seems rather a neat, rounded-up kind of time to me. 9.29 or 9.31 might have been more plausible. Anyway, it matters not.

First they take her away, weigh, clean and check her over. This was before the days when new-borns were placed straight on their mother's tummy, assisting that all-important bonding process. And in any case bonding was the last thing they wanted to encourage between a birth mother (as I was later to discover I'd be labelled) and this child destined for adoption. As it was, when they took her off for these things I hadn't the slightest idea when they'd bring her back – if indeed ever. I knew the intention was that I should have her with me for eight days, but at that point I felt so utterly unempowered that I don't even know I'd have had the will to fight if they'd said she'd already been taken away - given to more "suitable" parents. I certainly felt I had no *right* to question anything. These people were the 'experts' and I was nothing. No, I was less than nothing.

The inevitable barbarisms follow. I've been given an episiotomy, and the stitching job which follows is agony and deeply traumatising. Again, I presume that's just how things are - legs up in stirrups, indignity after indignity. I'm like a piece of meat and I can't say I ever truly recovered from that. Eventually I'm put onto a full ward with an extraordinary mix of other mothers: one's had a miscarriage; one suffered a stillbirth. Another has a miniscule premature baby in intensive care, where she spends most of her time when she's not on the ward crying. The baby's wrapped in silver foil, she tells us. They don't know if he'll live. Her heart is breaking. One or two of them seem to be straight-forward cases – if there *is* such a thing. I lie there, waiting, and still waiting. Finally my new-born daughter is brought to me.

I've never seen anything so beautiful. She takes me breath away. I am so very proud she's mine. For ages I gaze at her face, and then slowly I get to know the rest of her. I take the tiniest of fingers in mine – I've never touched a new-born before – and those tiny, tiny fingers....and these feet, with ten teeny weeny toes. Oh my god! I produced this baby. She's mine. I want to kiss every inch of this sweet-smelling bundle of loveliness. This is *my* child, my daughter.

Eight Days

In the bed next to me is Jane, seventeen years old and with her second child – soon to be adopted, as was her first. She's given pretty short shrift by many of the nurses, but she really doesn't appear to be that bothered by them. Her boyfriend comes to visit: he's not the father, but he's devoted to Jane, and she's outwardly philosophical about the whole adoption thing: they'll have their own baby soon, and then life will be perfect. That's what she says.

"Whatever you do, don't get attached to it," she warns. "I did last time, and it was hell. I'm not doing it this time! Just feed it, change it and put it back in the nursery."

"Her," I correct her, gazing at this beautiful baby girl.

"Her what?"

"It's a 'her'. She's a girl."

"Right."

"She's called Alison."

"Suit yourself."

Jane's a tough cookie.

Looking back, I guess she had to be. And I'm sure she knew what she was talking about. She was right, in a sense. I certainly made it harder than it needed to be. But I wouldn't have changed those eight days I had with my daughter for love nor money nor riches beyond my wildest imaginings.

The period of being in hospital with a new baby you know you have for only a few days is completely surreal. The word psychosis comes to mind: 'psyche' referring to the mind or the soul, and 'osis' meaning abnormality of some kind. I certainly can't describe the hundred and ninety-five hours I had with my daughter as normality of the mind or soul, not in any sense. I moved between stretches of incredible, quite literally fantastic, intimacy: the new mother with the most beautiful child in the world, here in her arms. The child she has carried, through all the stresses, for forty weeks….here, now, at her breast. But not quite at her breast. Bursting, running with a mother's milk, I was not allowed to breastfeed – not allowed. Fed pills to dry my milk, I suffered a physical as well as an emotional pain; soaking gowns, dripping breasts, the drying up took forever, each moment a reminder of what I wasn't permitted to do, the intimacy I wasn't allowed to develop.

This close, no further.

So I feed my daughter by bottle, and she feeds well, her appetite healthy. "Guzzle guzzle" the nurses call her, a healthy 8lbs 5 and growing by the day.

I bathe her, soft skin sliding precariously through my fingers, the bath set up beside my bed. And nappy after nappy teaches me that one's own child *always* smells sweet, whatever state they're in – maybe especially so if you know there will be nappies only for eight days and not a moment longer. It becomes not a chore, oddly, but a privilege.

What state of mind must this be, if not an abnormality of the mind, of the soul?

So I play at being Mummy. At some times it's an idyllic existence. Just me and Alison. And at others I cry myself hollow – locked in the toilet so no-one will see me, under my blankets at night in the vain hope my sobbing will go unheard. At least I'm left alone.

Jane in the next bed has that stream of visitors – brothers, a sister. Both sets of parents come too. They take pictures, each of them smiling proudly with the baby in turn, sitting on the edge of the bed, standing by the window with the sun streaming in.

No photos are taken of Alison, the better to forget as speedily as possible. Neither my mother nor my father comes to see their daughter with her first child; no gifts from them, not a single tear shed, neither of joy nor regret. A year later my parents will celebrate the arrival of their 'first grandchild' when Anne has her son. Legitimately.

But to this day I still cannot walk past a flower stall fragrant with freesias without being transported back to that ward in Freedom Fields. My sister arrived to see her niece, to welcome her, to love her, and to congratulate me, thrilled that her baby sister had produced such a beautiful child herself. And Peter, my loving brother, came too to celebrate - the proud uncle - as did Jeff. These were my visitors. These were the people to meet my child before she was taken away, given to new 'better' parents.

Night-times were special. At night-time the nurses insisted babies spend the dark hours separated from their mothers. New mothers needed their rest, the babies needed wakeful supervision – which was best provided by the nurses, well-slept and professional. But with only a hundred and ninety-five hours to spend with my baby, I wasn't going to let them separate us for nights at a time.

In the dead of night it was possible to sneak some time alone, a snatch of intimacy in the darkness, making believe we weren't in a hospital, weren't going to be parted, we were just like all the other 'proper' mothers and babies. I'd slide into the nursery unnoticed, and sit there with Alison in my arms. But there was always that chance a nurse would pass by and usher me to bed. More anxious moments; more nerves on end. Watching, holding my breath. On my last night I could bear it no longer. Creeping into the nursery, I lifted Alison gently from her cot, replacing her blankets in the same positions as before. Maybe they wouldn't notice she had gone. Movements kept to a minimum – she must *not* wake up - I carried her close to my breast, measured step by measured step back to the safety of the ward. Climbing back into bed, I wrapped the blankets around the two of us, her soft skin on my cheek, feeling her chest rise and fall with her tiny short breaths. Her warmth through her nightgown passed through to me, just where my heart lay. If time stood still, I'd hold her in my arms forever, smell her milky breath, feel the shallowness of her breathing...still breathing. I wouldn't put her down in case she stopped. This breath that began in me, that started with me and her dad. Breath he'll never hear, never feel. The baby he'll never see, never touch. But it's OK. It's OK. Feeling enough for both of us...for a whole world who'll never see her with me. Enough love for the whole world here, under this tiny head. In my breast. Hair so soft against my cheek...a tiny chick. Softest down in the whole world. Lay your head on my breast, my baby.

No, you mustn't suckle. They say I mustn't - too much bonding. We'll grow too close. Separating will be too hard, they

142

say. But they can't see the bond if it's invisible - and it's there, my love. It is there.

Mother time. Forbidden time. Magic hours before dawn, when anything seems possible. And before I know it, for the first time in a week I'm asleep. And we're playing – playing on a beach, building castles. And she is a fairy princess, and I'm a queen. And we're happy, together, in the sun in some faraway place.

And then I feel her being torn away. "What do you think you're doing, Susan!"

"Please!"

"It's dangerous for baby. And it is not good for you, Susan. You know that. Now come on; get some sleep. She's better off in the nursery. You know that. Stop this nonsense!"

My daughter lets out a primal cry. For her. For me. For every mother and child wrenched apart, over the centuries.

And then she's gone.

Leaving. Again

The day for us to leave comes around all too swiftly. Eight days that feel in one sense like a lifetime are over in the blinking of an eye. Miss Featherstone, my social worker, had always been a kind, sensitive lady who I'm convinced genuinely wanted to discover what it was that *I* wanted to happen. And now I believe that if I'd been able to say, "Of course I don't want you taking my baby! What do you think I am!" she would have done her utmost to make it happen. But there was no way she could have understood the throttling grip my mother had on our family, and no-one could possibly have conveyed to her the absolute terror I felt at the thought of crossing her. It just wasn't a discussion that was ever going to happen.

So kindly or not, the last person I wanted to see on that dreadful eighth day was the ageing Miss Featherstone, reassuringly smiling at me, reaching out to take my baby in her arms. My sister stood by her side, her heart close to breaking for what she knew I must be going through. For most of my life she, seven years older, had been a maternal presence in my life, holding me close, keeping me safe. Now there was nothing she could do to save me from what I had to face.

"I'll carry her," Miss Featherstone says. "It'll be best, I think."

Best? Best! What could possibly be 'best' about anything going on here! My sister takes my hospital bag. So I carry nothing, while Miss Featherstone carries my daughter, in a carry basket I think she must have bought especially for this occasion, this baby. But I wonder now just how many other babies would have been carried down in that same basket. Or was there a new one for each child, a freebie for the new parents? I hated that woman today. She stood for everything ripping my child away from me.

We seem to wait forever for the lift, my head throbbing as I fight back tears, every fibre screaming that I could run away....we could run away together. I could find somewhere to live, find a way to survive, hold onto my child, not let her go. I look straight ahead, steeling myself for the inevitable.

Don't think about it. Just don't think about it. It's a dream, a play. It's a part. It's not real.

The lift doors open and I say nothing, despite a silent cry deep inside. Stepping into that confined space with this compassionate, caring woman about to tear my life apart, I seem to be losing touch with reality, a fury rising like a tidal wave in me. How *dare* they! How can they!

No, don't feel this. Don't think about this, about any of this. It's not happening, not to you. This is happening to someone else.

And again I displace myself, hammering a lid on every scrap of emotion, knowing it will get me nowhere. I'll have to face my mother and none of this was of my choosing, none of it within my control.

My behaviour that day was a masterpiece in method acting. Stanislavski would have been impressed with me, immersing myself as I was in the character of a girl who really did believe it was, "best all round...best for the baby, best for you". I sit in the front of the car with Miss Featherstone. Anne sits in the back with the baby, already someone else's. Already so far away. Just look out of the window, watch the people out there. All those people with their normal lives doing normal things on this thirteenth day of the sixth month of nineteen hundred and seventy-two; a Tuesday like any other for most of them. A Tuesday like no other for me. For them life won't be significantly different tomorrow from today. For me life will never be the same again. Not without her. Not without my daughter.

We turn the corner into Anne's road, pulling up outside her house. Anne gets out of the car, coming around to help me. I step out; it's like we are all arriving at a funeral, mixed expectation and dread, all bottled up until the hymns start and the tears are allowed to flow.

Guide me, oh thou great redeemer...

Miss Featherstone steps out of the car now. Neither Anne nor I seem to know the rules of the game at this point. It is only she who knows the protocol. Do we take the baby out? Do I say goodbye? Is there a final kiss, after so so many in those freedom fields?

I look at the woman, pleading silently with my eyes. *"Please tell me it is a mistake. I can keep her. Ask me again. Ask me if this is what I want. Ask me now…in this instant. Ask me!"*

She half-smiles at me, trying to protect us all. "We won't bring baby in. Best not."

She's got a name! She's Alison. She's got a name!

And it's at that moment that I notice my parents' car a few houses along. They must be in the house. They'll come out. They'll see my baby, they'll hold her…and then they'll say, "Oh look, we've made a terrible mistake. Let's take her home." And that will be that, and we'll all be fine. It will have been a terrifying ordeal, and I will have learned just how much you risk when something like this happens, but it'll all be OK now. I'll have learned the lesson. I won't let this happen again. I swear I won't. I promise! Any minute now, they'll appear. Any minute.

"Are your parents here?" Miss Featherstone asks my sister gently, glancing into the back of the car. I can see it in her eyes – she's thinking the same as me. They'll come out, hold me, pick up their grandchild, take her in…

"Yes, they are. But they don't want to see the baby." I go back over the words in my head. *They don't want to see the baby.*

And my heart breaks. Because in those seven words my world entirely unravels.

Adoption

Adoption. Sounds easy. Sounds logical. A positive thing: *best for you; best for baby*.

But adoption is unlike anything else – at least, the way in was done in the seventies. Things have moved on somewhat now, but there are still so many of us out there who suffered – and *suffer* is the right word – from the system as it was before recent reforms. It's different from bereavement. There is no finality, no closure. There is serious unfinished emotional and psychological business following you around for the rest of your life. In this case, back in the seventies, eighties, nineties, the 'normal' state of affairs after the decree absolute was that a birth mother might spend the rest of her life having no idea whether her child was alive or dead.

For years after losing my daughter I visited my sister in Devon during holidays – first as a schoolgirl, then as an undergraduate, and eventually as a new (and then, later, an experienced) teacher. Visiting Plymouth city centre – whether Christmas shopping, or on the way for a late summer swim below the Hoe, or wading through the Spring sales – it was difficult not to be on the lookout for my daughter with her new parents, and to wonder what they themselves must be like. Not once did I walk through those streets, crowded in the summer with tourists, bleak and deserted in February half-term, not once did I walk through those streets without scouring faces, searching for something – anything – familiar in the eyes, the smile, the nose. It was hard at first, with babies under rain covers, wrapped deep under fleeces and blankets, hidden away. Later I would search for features resembling the one photograph Social Services had eventually sent me after a lot of badgering on my part. Or maybe there'd be a hint of me

147

in pictures of when I'd been a child, or a cross between the two perhaps.

As the years passed by I had finally to accept that we might even pass one another in the street and I'd fail to recognise her – my own flesh and blood. I wondered whether I might one day have held the door open for my own child in Debenhams or Smiths or the doctor's surgery I still sometimes had cause to visit when I was in Devon. I wouldn't have recognised her from Eve. Had I stood in the covered market beside this young woman, failing to recognise my own flesh and blood? Had we stood there at the fruit stall, held for a moment in its pool of light, an intimate interlude in our separate lives, me a grown woman and her the child I longed to find, to touch, to hold? The child I wanted to share my life with. Had we shared a brief thirty seconds before she'd gone again, a bagful of bananas and apples in her arms? And we wouldn't have exchanged a word.

Or worse. When a school trip from Devon was reported to have been tragically cut short with the coach involved in a collision, or a child had died on an activity holiday – I had given up the right to know whether it was my child when I had signed the decree absolute. No way to find out – what name would she have now – and no end to the dreadful possibilities. I found myself repeatedly in the darkest of places, my mind taking me where I'd best not go.

Birthdays were particularly peculiar occasions. To celebrate or not to celebrate, the annual question. In my second year at university my boyfriend found me in tears one night.

"Tell me." He thought it was over between us.

"It's not us," I tried to explain. "It's Alison's birthday, and..." I sobbed in his arms. "And I forgot...the whole day, I forgot."

He was bemused. I had a school-friend called Alison, and he thought I'd meant her. Why would he possibly think I was talking about anyone else? Of course he knew I'd had a child, but we'd never really talked about it and I don't think I'd even told him her name. So that was the night we talked until dawn, with me wrapped in his arms. For once I felt someone understood how I felt.

"We'll get her back," he said determinedly, stroking my face.

"We can't."

"Yes we can. We'll start looking into it tomorrow."

"It's not like that, Graham. I don't know where she is, no - but I don't have any rights either. You don't understand."

His naivety was charming, but less than practical, and it took some time to convince him that even if I could have found her, even if I'd had those rights birth mothers now have enshrined in law in most cases, it would be just as traumatic to rip a child away a second time from the family she'd know and love by now, away from where she'd feel safe. No, it wasn't going to happen.

He cried with me that night and held me so close I thought I'd melt into him, and for that birthday at least I felt I wasn't alone.

More often than not on her birthday, though, I'd wish my daughter a silent greeting, and try to convince myself she was better off where she was, that she'd have a better life than any she might have had with me. Better than living with a single teen mother going nowhere, and her growing up taunted with "Oi, bastard!" And there's no doubt she would have been – from some idiot, at least. No, there was no escaping that. And what could I have given her, I asked myself again. Compared with the comfortable middle-class home she had now, what could I have done for her? I would have had to quit school at fifteen with no qualifications and very limited prospects, and it had been absolutely clear my mother'd had no intentions of giving up work and raising *another* child. She said as much. I'd have been on benefits until Alison was at school and then I maybe could have found a job at AB Metals like my mother. Maybe. Job opportunities for unskilled, unqualified female labour in The Valleys back then, much as elsewhere, much as now, were few and far between. And even if I'd been lucky enough to find one, the pay would have been a pittance in those days before the minimum wage and equality laws.

No, she was much better off with her engineer dad and hairdressing mum with her own salon. And her brother – she had a brother too. Yes, I knew that. That much detail I had from the adoption agency. Just enough to persuade me I was doing 'the right thing'; just enough to make it patently clear I couldn't compete. Just enough to make me feel I'd have been letting her down even to try to hold onto her.

But her eighteenth birthday, her coming-of-age, was something else altogether. So momentously significant, for her and for me, I knew.

Back in 1990, when my daughter turned eighteen, the law prevented the birth parent finding any details about their child. But once she would come of age, Alison could trace me. And it was going to be a very easy, swift and simple process. If she went to Plymouth Social Services and asked for her file, she would be halfway home. Home. Where the heart is, and always had been. I knew there was a requirement for her to receive some counselling, and of course I could see why the agencies had to make sure she was in the right state of mind. But I was confident it wouldn't take long. I had absolutely no doubt whatsoever, not for a single moment, that she'd present herself on her 18th birthday at the door of the relevant department, request her file, and we'd be off. I even thought she might have gone through the counselling process in the run-up to her birthday, so we could be reunited at the earliest possible moment. It hadn't even occurred to me that anything could be otherwise.

My sister still lived in the same house, the house I'd lived in for most of my pregnancy; the address I'd filled in on the adoption papers. That would clearly be the starting point of our journey back to each other. Anne knew I couldn't wait to have my daughter back in my life, so there we were.

The day arrived. Almost time to start healing those wounds. I wasn't expecting miracles, but at least we could start getting to know each other now after a lifetime apart. Her lifetime apart from her 'real' mother, and what felt like a lifetime for me, too. I felt so very alone over this whole adoption thing.

As it happened, I'd been invited to supper by a friend, a teaching colleague, on the night of Alison's coming of age. I turned up with strawberries and a bottle of vintage champagne. Never one to turn down a good drink, Carol was nonetheless surprised at my extravagance when there was ostensibly nothing in particular to celebrate, other than it being a Tuesday night and the fact that we weren't spending it marking endless essays!

"Actually there's a reason for the champagne, Carol." I twisted the bottle in my hand, easing the cork out with the intention of not spilling a drop. It was a skill I'd mastered early on at uni, but with cava rather than the real stuff.

"What's that, then?"

Pop!

"It's my daughter's eighteenth."

My heart was pounding, saying the words, but even so I made her wait while I poured. My friend looked at me, astonished. We'd known each other some years. I knew all about *her* children, but what was this?

"Daughter! What daughter?"

What was I talking about? She knew I was desperate to have kids. She knew I'd been through years of IVF. But a daughter!

I'd kept Alison's existence a secret from most people throughout my life. Or so I'd thought. It was quite amusing to discover, some years later, that half of Mount had worked out why I'd been sent away to stay with my sister: the 'nervous disorder' bit had never washed. It didn't take a rocket scientist, after all.

But that had been Mount, where I'd played the vanishing act, and nothing after all was ever private there for long. This on the other hand was Cambridge, and I'd only moved here as a graduate. There'd have been no reason why anyone would imagine I'd had a child all those years before. Why on earth would they?

And so the story began. First over the champagne I'd brought – toasting absent loved ones and my daughter in particular – then over a Bourgogne and finally, I seem to recall, over brandy and chocolates. It was a night to remember and a hangover from hell the next day in college. Sod it! Your daughter only reached 18 once, for godsake!

For weeks afterwards I rushed to pick up the post, *knowing* she'd be in touch. I told myself I'd been rash in thinking it could be instantaneous; I reflected on how *long* the counselling process can be, and how painfully slowly the wheels of bureaucracy grind. But after months of waiting and day after day no letter, no phone call, I finally had to accept she wasn't going to be in touch. Not then, and maybe not ever.

And still, despite her adult status, I had no right to information which might help *me* trace *her*, no matter how desperate I was (and believe me, I *was*) to find my daughter. Like a slow awakening it was, the light appearing first as the early traces of dawn creeping through a chink in the curtains, eventually flooding the room and blinding me. Yesterday I'd thought I'd known where I was going: my daughter would write; we'd meet; it would if we were very lucky be happy ever after.

But that was yesterday when I'd thought I'd known what was ahead. And this was today, when I couldn't see the path in front of my feet, the glare of reality blindingly painful. I may never see my child again.

"Mam"

When did I stop calling her 'Mam'? Not in directly addressing her, I don't mean that. I continued doing that until the end of her life. No, I mean in the third person, with my brother and sister in particular. For some years to Anne and Peter she had become 'Mother' – not as in 'my mother'. Just 'Mother'. There was something decidedly distancing about it, stripping away any possibility of intimacy. 'Mother.' Strange, isn't it. A word, a role, at the very core of my identity, the essence of who I am. The thing I'm most proud to call myself: *Hi, I'm Ben's mother.* Proud to say it. Privileged to be it. And yet, used as a name for our own maternal parent it distanced the three of us from her for the last couple of decades of her life.

So when did I stop calling her 'Mam'?

Too long ago to remember, that's when. And too long ago to remember why. Because Anne and Peter called her Mother, I think. Sometime after my father had died. Or maybe not. Who knows. It really doesn't matter anymore. The same as the wording on her grave stone. *In Memory of Ruth Jenkins.* Not *In Loving Memory.* Just *Memory.* Why? And who decided? Me and Anne? It was we who went to the funeral director. Or the three of us? Did we all decide? And for whom? And why do I find that stone so very hard to look at, standing as it does, the only stone engraved *In Memory* amongst all the others , *In Loving memory…Sadly Missed…Love you Forever.* One word. *Loving.* And we felt for some reason – for many reasons? – unable to say it. It breaks my heart now.

So when did I stop calling her 'Mam' - to Anne and Peter? Who knows. Who cares.

I do. I care. Now I care.

My mother's ashes were buried in Mount Cemetery in the plot she'd paid for decades earlier, the payment unbeknown to any of us three children at the time. We found out when we opened an envelope she'd given Jeff years ago, to be opened on the event of her death. She'd had a plot all lined up. Her ashes lie less than half a mile up the road from her beloved *Fairlight Villa,* the house where she'd last lived in Mount; the house they'd moved to while I was down in Plymouth having my daughter. That way they'd never have to face the neighbours again once I was home. New neighbours, new identity. I'd just been 'away', staying at my sister's for a week or two. That's what the shiny new neighbours were told.

Fairlight Villa: where, on that fateful New Year's morning when my mothers' life had toppled, spun and done a backflip, finding Dad dead in bed aged forty-nine. Two weeks later, after a funeral neither she nor I attended, she had packed a case, left Fairlight, and gone to stay with Anne and Jeff in Plymouth for a while. She was never to return.

....neither she nor I attended...

Her husband's funeral. My father.

Neither she nor I attended. At the time I didn't question it. I was in shock. She was in shock. She said she didn't feel strong enough to face the funeral and no-one managed to persuade her (maybe no-one tried – I can't say), so I stayed with her, and we made sandwiches for everyone's return. We made sandwiches. While busloads of my dad's workmates turned out to pay their respects, to say farewell, to take their leave, we made sandwiches. Cheese and tomato, egg and salad cream, John West salmon and cucumber, just like the beach. Crusts cut off, a bit fancy for a special occasion.

Neither she nor I attended. And it didn't strike me as odd. It would have been the first funeral I'd have been to; I had no idea what was right and what was downright extraordinary. So as I spread more butter on yet another loaf of Sunblest, and the only duty I felt was to make sure my mother was alright, that she was busy, that she kept her mind off why we were the only two in the house. That she kept her mind off it. Her husband's funeral. My father.

So that's all I remember of Dad's funeral. John West. Only the best.

And when it came to her own funeral arrangements, my mother didn't choose to have her ashes buried near his. Nor with her own mother, despite longing to be reunited with her. She chose to have them buried in Mount cemetery with her youngest brother, Tom, less than half a mile from Fairlight Villa.

She lived to reach eighty-one, my mother. A good age. She lived to meet my daughter, her grand-daughter, whose adoption she had engineered all that time ago - not that you could say she ever really developed any kind of relationship with her. But that was maybe too much to expect of anyone, let alone this damaged woman.

She lived a long life, though, and she stayed physically very fit. Just days before the stroke that eventually killed her, she'd travelled into Plymouth by bus, exactly as she did most days, going into town to spend time with the purveyors of fruit and veg on the market stalls. She often talked about them like long-lost friends, regaling me with the details of the crises in their lives. I heard more about them than I did about members of her own (my own) family. I'd always regarded this as yet another of her displacement activities, failing as she did to have any kind of meaningful conversation with any of us – god forbid she should ask about *my* life, how *I* was. No, that was far too threatening, far too close to the dreaded intimacy. Better to spend every waking moment talking about people I'd never met, never planned to meet, and had absolutely no desire to meet.

"They love having me down the market. They really do. They bring a stool over, and it's 'Sit down there, Ruth. Let's get you a cup of tea, Ruth'. I was telling them about Ben being in the school play the other day." She could carry on endlessly like this on the phone, but I'd never been able to imagine these people...if indeed they actually existed anywhere other than in her mind. And I certainly couldn't begin to imagine these people having one iota of genuine interest about what was happening three hundred miles away in the life of a child they'd never met.

How wrong was I.

Days after she died a beautiful bouquet arrived at my sister's house as we finalised the funeral arrangements, tying bunches of daffodils with her favourite-coloured green ribbon.

"To our darling Ruth. We will miss you. From all the crew at the market."

Anne and I looked at each other, speechless. It was true. It was all true. She really had spent hours at the market, and they really had loved having her there. They'd pulled up the stool and they'd asked about Ben. Two of them even took time off from the stall to come to her funeral - almost the only people outside immediate family.

"She used make us laugh so much," they smiled sadly. "She was a scream, your mum. You must really miss her."

We racked our brains, trawling our memories, trying to recall times when we might have seen her in a similar light. I had a few occasions – most of them at our home in Cambridge, or the night of the first moon landing, when she'd bumped into Jeff on the stairs in the dark as she'd climbed out of bed to come down to find out how the mission was progressing, just as he was making his way up to tell us all they'd landed safely. Meeting on the stairs in pitch black as they'd both crept around silently, they'd scared the living daylights out of each other and then collapsed on the stairs in hysterics, trying to muffle their laughter like school kids.

But these moments were few and far between, and increasingly rare as the pressures of living a stone's throw away from each other with a deteriorating relationship and a cart load of history took their toll. Nonetheless moments of fun there were, and I'd be devastated now if I'd *never* seen that side of her. For these people on the market though this funny, zany sweet old woman was who our mother *was!*

So no, little could keep Mother from getting on that bus and nipping in to the market – right up until the day she died, practically. Nor, thankfully, did she travel far down that road of losing her mind. She'd surprised Anne one day telling her she'd eaten a pear and the skin had been so tough she'd had to spit it out; when Anne looked in

156

the bin, she found an avocado stone – but then, it *was* called a pear! But as an octogenarian she was doing fine mentally if not psychologically and emotionally. Until, that is, Anne called in one day as she did most days, and found her in a strange state, disorientated and incoherent, walking first upstairs then downstairs then up again. Alarmed, Anne called Jeff, and they rang the doctor.

"Should we call an ambulance?"

"She's in her eighties, Mrs Morgan, and what you're describing sounds like a sudden deterioration into dementia. It's not what they'll class an emergency, so she will be low priority, I'm afraid." *Thank you NHS.* "You'd be quicker waiting for me to come over as soon as I finish surgery. I won't be long."

But he *was* long, and meanwhile Anne was becoming increasingly alarmed, Mother now lying on her bed, trying quite literally to climb the wall. Anne called me.

"You need to call an ambulance," I said. She repeated the doctor's words. "Shall I come?" I asked, sitting down, all the implications racing through my head. I was a resident housemistress at a boarding school, and it was the day before forty-five teenage girls would arrive back from their Christmas holidays for the start of term, followed the next morning by another twenty. Things would need to be put in place, and fast.

Hindsight is a marvellous thing, but Anne couldn't be sure how serious it was until the doctor arrived. "No. Just wait until the doctor's seen her," she told me, "but have a bag ready."

I drove the three hundred miles to her house in three hours flat, ready to justify it to any police officer, ready to pay any fine and have any points on my license. When I arrived at 1am Mother was in Derriford Hospital, unconscious and on a drip. Adrenalin coursed through my veins as we walked towards the main entrance in one of those schizophrenic moments, a "Run….don't run" battle in your head, shattering brain cells by the bucket load. Derriford is a bleak, godforsaken place high up on a hill above the outskirts of the city. Four hundred feet above sea level in an area known a hundred years ago as Knackers Hole, it's within spitting distance of Ma-John and just below Plymouth airport, which itself runs alongside the Wrigley's factory. My memory tells me it's impossible flying out of there without being overwhelmed by what smells like toothpaste. That night all I got was a whiff of Benson and Hedges as we made our way through the door, passing the visitors to the heart transplant unit grabbing a quick fag break before heading back in to be with their next of kin.

A depopulated night-time hospital is an oddly comforting place to be. People move quieter, though no slower, than during daylight hours. The café is closed, chairs upside down on tables; the shop protects its wares with metal shutters lest anyone try to break in for a packet of hobnobs. We don't take the lift. I hate them at the best of times – another fear I shared with my mother – but at times of high anxiety I just cannot do them. I've been known to walk up five flights before a routine appointment because I'm so unnerved.

So there we are, my big sister and me silently gelling our hands side by side before ringing the bell to gain access to the ward. I rub the gel in far more than necessary, unable to keep my hands still. My feet move in sympathy. Greeted by the nurse – they were all, without exception, fabulous, as were the doctors – Anne smiles, "Hallo. We're here to see my mother, Ruth Jenkins. This is my sister, Susan." She doesn't say *baby* sister, although I feel it.

"Hallo." The nurse smiles back sympathetically, recognising her from earlier. Anne knows where she is going, and before I know it, we're stepping through the door to the small side room which will be the last room my mother ever sees.

She looks tiny. Tiny and fragile, her white roots shining on her scalp, Nice'n'Easy still colouring the rest. Forty years of Nice'n'Easy, the brand with the strap line, "The closer she gets, the better you look." The closer I get, the less I see of the woman I hugged before driving home after Christmas, just weeks ago, her hand patting my back: *that's enough of a show of emotion, now; this close, no closer.* The closer I get, the more I nearly disintegrate. The closer I get, the stronger I have to be – for her. I want to climb on that bed, hold her whole body close to mine and tell her I forgive her. I forgive her for taking my child away; I forgive her for destroying my father's life; I forgive her for driving wedge after wedge after wedge between this us in this family. I forgive her – for everything. Because she never intended it. She never intended any of it. She just couldn't do it any other way.

But I stand beside her bed, I take her hand in mine, and I kiss her cheek. Stroking her hair nice and easy, I whisper gently, close to her. "It's alright, Mam. It's Susan. It's alright. I'm here now. It's OK, Mam. I'm here."

Not 'Mother'. Mam.

The Call

"I think you'd better sit down. Your daughter's trying to find you." Words I'd long since resigned myself never to hear.

"What? What are you saying?" It should make perfect sense. It makes none.

"Your sister's called, and says your daughter's been in Mount, trying to find you. She's called Helen."

"I don't understand." What's he talking about? Helen? Who's Helen? What's this about my daughter?

"Her adoptive parents called her Helen," he smiles. Something computes.

"No, I don't mean...I mean….why's she in Mount? How does my sister know? I mean…"

"She tried to find you – at the address you gave Social Services when you had her. She went back to the address in Mount, where you were living when you were fifteen."

"But…" I want every question answered *right* now, but I can't even find the questions.

"And people remembered you, but they said your family'd moved away, to somewhere else in Mount."

"We did, yes. They moved. When I was in Plymouth my parents sold up in Miskin and moved to Aberdare Road – the other end of Mount. I came home to a new house."

What you have to realise here is that Miskin and Mount are like your right hand and your right-hand fingers. Miskin is *in* Mountain Ash, so the chances of achieving my mother's much-desired anonymity by moving house were just about as close to zero as you can get.

"Helen tried to find you in the phone directory, and…"

"We didn't have a phone."

"…and then she went to see the vicar…"

"Huh!" Fat lot of good that would have been.

"…but he couldn't find anything, so he suggested she went in to the local paper."

"The Leader?"

"I don't know. She didn't say."

"It would have been." It was all starting to make sense.

"And she asked if she could put an advert in, but they were interested in her story so they ran a front page story."

"Front page! My mother'll go ballistic."

Bert laughs, welling up. "So what do you think of that, then? Your daughter! Hey?"

And then the enormity of it hits me. My *daughter. My* daughter! I'm going to be in touch with *my* daughter.

"She's alive," I say quietly.

"Yes."

And then the flood gates open. She hasn't died in a coach crash without me knowing…there's been no tragedy on a school trip, no being washed down a river or falling down a cliff. She's alive. And I'm going to meet her. She is flesh, and she's blood. My daughter's real, no longer just a dream. I collapse in Bert's arms.

"Oh my god!" My husband holds me close, the pain and the joy and the fears and the hopes all wrapped up together in one enormous mélange of emotions. And finally I'm doing something I haven't dared allow myself to do for twenty-one years: I'm letting my feelings out.

There follow a couple of days of to-ing and fro-ing. My brother-in-law's sister, who still lives in Mount, had contacted the paper to say she knows me. She'd obtained an address for 'Helen' (how strange to think of Alison with a different name after all these years), and my sister had written to say, "I'm your mother's sister, Anne. I know she'll want to be in touch with you. How do you want her to contact you?" She'd had to wait for a letter back, but now I have a phone number in front of me. Helen has asked if I'll call that night. It's the evening before her twenty-first birthday.

I return from the performance of the play around 10.30, hardly able to believe that exactly twenty-one years ago, to the day, I'd been in Freedom Fields Hospital in labour with the daughter I'm now about to talk with for the first time.

After the show tonight, as each night, the company holds a post-show discussion with the audience. Every night practically every member of the audience stays, so engaged are they with the play and so keen to discuss the politics of adoption.

Tonight as every night there is the inevitable question about the real-life story: are you back in touch with your daughter? But tonight there's no well-rehearsed answer about the obstacles created by the current adoption legislation and the fact that the search can only be initiated by the child. Tonight I'm able to say, "I'm off home in a minute to speak to her for the very first time. I've got her number in my pocket here. So come again tomorrow night and I'll tell you what her voice sounds like." They're speechless. You can feel the excitement in the room. I continue smiling, "So I'm sure you'll forgive me if we don't take too many questions just now."

There is warm, supportive laughter. But of course that's the last thing I should be telling them if I want any chance of a quick get-away: now they want the whole story, because now a new real-life drama's unfolding – and they're a part of it. How had she had found me, what were my expectations, my hopes…. how was I feeling? It's as if just for that moment we're all locked into something quite, quite extraordinary. And in a sense we are, because what might have been such a private moment for most birth mothers as they're made whole again by the reuniting with their child, for us was such a public affair. My writing of the play, my commitment to giving women's experiences a voice, my determination that women's lives should be centre stage – these things had brought me to where I now found myself: to being the public property of some curious and caring individuals who'd been profoundly moved by my story thus far. And now they want to know there'll be a happy ending.

"Enough questions," someone says from the front row. "Let the woman go. She's got a phone call to make." And everyone laughs warmly, then the applause begins.

"Thank you. Thank you so much."

My hands are cold and shaking as I dial the number, even though I'm at home on a warm summer's evening. It rings for what feels like a lifetime. Please let someone answer. Please. My heart pounds against my chest wall. Large intake of breath, and a measured breath out. From the sound I could easily have been suffering labour pains.

"You OK?" Bert asks, beside me. He takes my hand.

"Yeah, fine. It's ringing."

After some time – probably not long, but time is elastic at times like this (*are* there any other times like this!) - a woman's voice answers.

"Hallo?" Time stops.

"Hallo, is that Helen?"

"No. I'll just call her for you. Is that Sue?"

"Yes, it is." I'm breathless. It's been a long day. A long life.

"Just hang on a minute, love. She knows you're calling."

And in the distance I hear the same voice calling what sounds like up the stairs.

"Helen. Sue's on the phone." Silence. It feels eternal as Bert watches me, expectant. Then I hear the phone being picked up. And I hear her voice. For the first time ever I hear my daughter's voice.

"Hallo?" Nothing will ever be this sweet.

"Hi." It's all I can say. I'm determined not to break down.

"Hiya!"

"This is really strange," I manage to say. And we both laugh. And I can't explain it, but I feel immediately like I've known this young woman all my life.

We do the stuff we *can* do by phone, which isn't a lot. Where do you live? She's in Wolverhampton....Was that her mum? No, her landlady; she and Martin are in digs. Martin's her boyfriend.....Yes, I'm married, to Bert.....No, I don't have any other children. Not yet....I live in Cambridge.....Yes, I did realise it was her birthday tomorrow....Yes, I knew it was her twenty-first. Was she planning anything?..... And the weekend, was she doing anything special? (*Clubbing should have been predictable, given that I was teaching A Level students and knew their lifestyles pretty well*)....Yes, yes I *was* doing something special this weekend, actually. I was directing a play I'd written. It's about her. It was on for the last time tomorrow, and I wondered if she wanted to see it....No, there weren't plans for it be on anywhere else. Not yet, anyway...... That was a pity, but no of course I understood.

I'd been expecting her to have something planned for her twenty-first….Yes, I'd love to meet her. I can't wait…..OK, a couple of weeks then, if she's not free until then…No, of course I understand. *(I'm gutted.)*

She's heading off out with some friends shortly to see her birthday in, and has to go in a minute. But there's one thing I need to tell her before we put the phone down. Better out than in, and I have no idea how she'll feel about it.

"Helen, I need to tell you something."

"Right?"

"I'm pregnant." There. I've said it.

"Right."

"*Very* pregnant."

"Right."

"I just thought you should know."

"Right. That's fine." And it really does sound like it is. "I mean it's great! OK. I need to go and party. I've got people waiting."

"OK. Will I speak to you soon? Can I call you tomorrow? To wish you Happy Birthday."

"That would be nice, yeah – but not too early!" She laughs.

"No, OK. And can I have your address? In case I want to send something?" So my daughter gives me an address in the West Midlands. And with that she's gone. I put the phone down, slightly stunned.

"So?" Bert looks at me, all smiles. "How's that then? You've spoken with your daughter." And he moves to hug me.

"Hang on," I hug him and move too quickly away. "I just need to ring Interflora."

"You sending her flowers?"

"A red rose for every birthday I've missed."

The phone rings early on Saturday morning – maybe not as early as it feels, but I've barely slept and I'm just drifting off so it feels like the middle of the night. Bert reaches out from bed and picks it up, sleepily. I've kept him awake too, struggling to get comfortable in both body and mind. I stuff the pillow over my head. It's too light; it's too noisy; it's too damned early to bloody well speak to anyone!

"Oh, hi....yeah, hang on. I'll give you Sue." He passes it over. "It's for you."

If it's one of the company I'll shoot them. If I can see straight. They know I need my sleep right now!

"Hallo?"

"Hi. It's Helen."

"Hi!" I'm wide awake suddenly, sitting up.

"It's not too early is it?"

"No. No, it's fine. We were awake already," I lie.

"Only, me and Martin have been talking, and I can't wait a couple of weeks. Is it still alright if we come down today?"

My heart soars. "Oh please. I didn't dare ask."

"And is your play still on?"

That Picture Of You

So here I am on a Saturday afternoon in early June, pacing up and down the sitting room waiting for a young woman – twenty-one, to be precise – to walk past my window and knock our door. I'd never really believed before this afternoon that people really do pace up and down, but here I am doing it so I suppose they must. And why do I think she will walk past the window? She might come from the other direction, in which case she'll just arrive at the front door. But parking's easier around the corner, which *would* bring her past the window. Not that she'll know about the parking. In any case she *might* find a space just up the road, in which case she'd just arrive at the door.

My mind won't stand still. Nor will my feet. So my whole body's on the move. The baby is too, picking up my adrenalin.

"Come and sit down."

"I can't. I'm OK. Really." I'm clearly driving Bert up the wall.

"Shall I have a blow?"

Bert's sax lies on the piano, and he has been itching to pick it up, but he's had to make do with drumming his sticks on his knee since he got back from Strawberry Fair where he played with a jazz band earlier. His drumming's driving me up the wall. I'd much rather he blew the sax.

"Yes, do love."

"Will you hear the door if they knock?"

"I'm sure I will." You *bet* I will!

"I'll go upstairs if you like."

"No, I'm fine. Honestly."

So he blows the sax. He rushed back frantically from the Fair to be here with me when they arrive. It's after three now, and he was

166

back for noon because Helen said they'd be here sometime this afternoon. Taking it literally that 'afternoon' means any time *after noon*, I knew that realistically one o'clock was the earliest they'd make it, and even that would have been pushing it. In fact, it wasn't realistic at all. But I was just willing them to arrive, and Bert had insisted he'd get back for twelve to make sure I wasn't on my own. In any case, he certainly didn't want to miss this momentous occasion.

Another young couple walk past the window, but I know instantly it's not her. With one or two people I haven't been so sure, and I held my breath to see if there was a knock at the door. This couple was a definite no, though.

Bert plays a Lester Young song I recognise but don't know the name of. It's not the one we had at our wedding, *These Foolish Things*. I hope she likes music.

I've booked them into a hotel. We've only got a two up, two down, and one of those has the cot in it. It's only one-and-a-half-up really, so there wouldn't have been space for a couple even if we hadn't put the cot in. Another part of me also thinks we need to take this slowly. We need to get to know each other first before they stay.

Another young woman walks past, but she's on her own so it can't be them. There'll two of them. But Martin could be parking the car, so it could be her, in that case. But she'd wait for him - especially today, coming here. How do I know that? Maybe that's not what they do.

There's a knock at the door.

"Love!" I call to Bert to put his sax down, my heart racing madly. He doesn't hear me first time so I call again. "Bert!" He rushes over, his sax slung around his neck still.

"Are they here?"

He follows me, excited as a child, to the front door, letting me be the one to open it. Through the frosted glass window I see what appears to be the figure of a young person. Opening the door I take a deep breath, steadying myself.

"Hallo," smiles the sweet-looking twenty-something brunette in front of me. "Do you have a few minutes to talk about The Bible?"

Bloody Jehovah's Witnesses! Or maybe she wasn't, but I wasn't interested in finding out.

"Do you know what, right now I probably do. But I'd rather not. I don't mean to be rude, but I'm waiting for someone. Somebody else."

"We're all waiting for somebody, though, don't you think?"

"I doubt very much you're waiting for the same person or with the same excitement as I am. Believe me." And I turn, leaving her with Bert. She persists.

"Oh but, that's where you're wrong."

"I don't think so," says Bert. "Goodbye. Sorry to do this." And he closes the door gently but firmly.

Last time we had Jehovah's witnesses he was just out of the bath and he answered the door in his pants. They too were young women, and when semi-naked Bert invited them in - as he would with JWs in those days, in the belief that the more time they spent with him (a confirmed atheist) the less damage they could be doing elsewhere – the two girls beat a hasty retreat, the word 'perve' muttered up a sleeve. Maybe not as charitable as one might have expected from the godly.

I put the kettle on, and we sit for some time with the ubiquitous tea for Bert and raspberry leaf for me, eyes glued to the window of our small terraced house in the bohemian part of Cambridge. I can concentrate on nothing.

And then they pass. A young man with shoulder-length curly hair, almost ringlets, and a young, shorter woman by his side. Helen's father had been shorter than me. White blonde hair, fine as a new-born, and eyes green as new-season fresh peas. At school he'd been a sprinter. I'd watched him run at County Athletics meets, and he'd played for the school's first rugby fifteen despite being only sixteen. He'd potentially been a serious sportsman, but sadly other things got in the way. His father's premature death had been the start of a downward drift.

Passing my window now was a young woman with the same unmistakable hair, behaving in the same unmistakable way, flying in the lightest of breezes.

"That's them," I say.

"How do you know?"

"I just know."

But we sit and wait, just in case. For moments there is no knock and I begin to doubt myself – but just a little. And then, finally, it comes - firm and strong. No messing about. No question of not being heard. This is someone determined to announce she is here. This person has waited some long, long time to be able to knock on that door.

And me? I have waited an eternity – her whole life - to hear it.

I calmly put my mug down. This time my breathing is fine; my heart feels right, no racing, no bursting, just…right. I can't explain it; it's just how it was.

I turn the latch and swing the door open, bright sunlight flooding in.

We both smile broad smiles.

"Hallo," I say. It feels simultaneously inadequate and totally right.

"Hiya! I'm Helen. But I guess you know that."

"I know that, yes." We both laughed. Bert cries, and laughs, and cries some more.

And we stand at the door, me and my daughter, just looking at each other for a moment.

She speaks first.

"So what do we do now?"

"Can I hold you?" I ask.

And she holds me, and I her. I never want to let go.

Women talk of losing a child to adoption as being like having a limb chopped off. Now I knew how it felt to have one restored. The only way I can describe it is that I felt whole again - instantly. And in a way that I hadn't even fully realised I'd felt amputated before. It really was like part of me had been returned. I described it at the time as being like having an arm sewn back on. I felt complete.

We sit on the sofa, Helen and me, next to each other, almost touching and sometimes not even almost. There are hugs, and hand-holding, and more hugs, and stroking her hair. And looking. We are transfixed by each other's features.

"You've got your father's eyes."

"They're the same shape as yours," Bert interjects.

"But they're the same colour as her father's. And his sister's. She had the same colour eyes – and hair. Really blond."

"This is bottle," she laughs.

"It still makes you look like him."

"But she's got your nose. Definitely."

"And I can see where I got my boobs from!" she explodes with laughter. "I never understood where these came from. I used to look at my mum and my gran and think, 'Well, it's not you two!' Now I know: it's your fault!"

"I've never been worried where they came from, to be honest!" jokes Martin.

But most of all, there's talking…so much talking. It's like she wants to tell me everything in one massive out-breath. About her mum and her dad, her brother and grand-parents and uncles and aunts – this whole family who've seen my child grow up. I keep having consciously to disengage emotionally, because there's too much here already that's too painful to hear. But at the same time I want - I need - to hear it, and she's desperate to pour it all out.

Yes, she's always known she was adopted, as long back as she can remember. Her parents – good people – told her she was special, that they chose her because she was special. And yet as a child on the beach she played at being locked up in a castle, her sandcastle, looking out to sea and pretending her real mother was a princess far away across the sea, and that one day she'd come and rescue her.

"That was my fravourite game," she says. She's never been able to say *favourite* without the extra letter.

Then out comes the photo album.

"This is my mum; this is dad, and my brother. That was our caravan in Cornwall, on my birthday, and that was my nana. This is Christmas when I was three, and this….."

So many people; so many memories; so many photographs. And every one a significant moment that I've missed in my daughter's life – time we'll never get back, memories I wasn't part of. So much I haven't shared. I swallow back everything I'm in danger of feeling. *No, don't cry. You mustn't cry. This has to be a happy day. Don't think about it. They're just photos. Just hold on. No tears. Not today.*

Then suddenly and for no apparent reason Bert leaps to his feet, disappearing upstairs. He almost trips on the stairs in his haste, not wanting to miss a moment of this catching up on a life I've missed out on.

"Wait a minute!" he shouts, taking them two at a time. We hear him thudding across the landing, over to the corner of the bedroom. Drawers being opened and shut, and the odd expletive in Dutch. Then a more satisfied grunt, and the speedy footsteps back again, and another near trip off the bottom step. I have no idea what's going on.

He has something in his hand - a small piece of paper or card. Holding it out, he hands it to Helen with a great beam on his face.

At first I can't see what he's brought, but Helen has put her album down beside her feet, and Bert stands over her now, proud of his idea and the fact that he's pulled it off, finding this in the clutter of our bedroom drawers.

"Is that me?" she asks him, and I can see now that it's a photograph. The only photograph I've ever had of my baby daughter. The photograph I'd had to chase and chase Social Services to send to me, desperate that I might forget her face.

"Yes," he says gently. "That's the only thing Sue's had, all these years – that picture of you."

And she looks at it closely this time, and then she looks at me in disbelief.

"Is that true?"

"Yes." I can barely speak now, the word choking me as the pain, so tightly contained until now, sweeps up from the depths of my very soul.

"Is that really all you've had?" I can see the look in her eyes, her father's eyes...the eyes I've never forgotten from the moment I lost her.

And that's it; that's the moment I break down, shoulders heaving, my face in my hands. Yes, it was all I'd had. It was all I'd feared I'd *ever* have, that one picture of a baby.

"Oh, come here." My daughter wraps me in her arms. "Don't cry. Come on. I'm here now. You've got *me*. I'm here. Look, I'm here. Come on. Don't cry."

Half A *Million* Women

From the wings I hear the theatre filling to capacity. The rest of the cast are readying themselves in the Green Room, but I'm alone behind the black tabs, waiting for my lighting cue. Those last few moments before stepping on stage fill different people with a whole array of emotions depending on so many factors, but for me tonight is nothing less than extraordinary; extra-ordinary indeed. The thrill of performing, yes, but this was performing a song which for me encapsulated the most traumatic experience of my life, and I was about to sing it as the opening of my raw emotional autobiographic play, in front of the child I'd been forced to give up a lifetime ago. There proudly in the middle of the front row sits my daughter, twenty-one today.

Years before, I'd had singing lessons. Having grown up immersed in song, I'd tried to keep up my singing in choirs. I'd sung at The Royal Albert Hall with a thousand Welsh voices, competed in singing festivals, sung the odd bit of jazz in various places. But now I found myself in the wings waiting to sing the hardest song of my entire life.

I am the one who will start the show, sitting in a rocking chair on a bare stage, singing 'a capella' in a single spot - not even a backing instrument to support me. Performance adrenalin piles on top of the emotions of the real-life drama unfolding before me right now as I wait in the wings for the signal to go. There is no going back.

Our technician takes down the house lights; the audience come to a swift hush. The stage is entirely dark as I make my way silently into position centre-stage. As the spotlight overhead rises in intensity, I gently rock in my chair for some moments, eyes closed, hands resting on my heavily pregnant tummy. The rocking slows to a halt. Once completely still, I open my eyes, meeting the gaze of the audience (I don't dare look at my daughter), and I sing – one voice, clear and soft, in a minor key:

> *Hush little baby don't say a word*
> *Mama's gonna buy you a mocking bird*
> *And if that mocking bird don't sing*
> *Mama's gonna buy you a diamond ring*
> *And if that diamond ring turns to brass*
> *Mama's gonna buy you a looking glass*
> *And if that looking glass gets broke*
> *Mama's gonna buy you a billy goat*
> *And if that billie goat falls down*
> *You'll still be the sweetest little baby in town*
> *So hush little baby, don't say a word*
> *Mama's gonna buy you a mocking bird.*
> *Hush little baby don't you cry*
> *Mama's gonna stay right by your side.*

And then I stand and walk to sit, as I have every night, in the centre of that front row, watching my story unfold. Night after night you could hear a pin drop as the scene unfolded, but this night is different. This night finds me sitting next to Helen, sharing this performance of our own drama, holding hands in that tiny intimate theatre in a back-street in Cambridge.

The play ends with words I'd written for another character in the play, another young birth mother:

I like to think I'll meet him one day. I bet I will. I can feel it in my bones. My mum reckons he'll get in touch when he's eighteen. I've even kept a lock of his hair. He was so blond.

I look at my daughter, here beside me. So is she.

Another Birth

Nine weeks after meeting my first-born I go into labour with my second child on a Friday, late morning. "Keep moving," I've learned in my ante-natal classes. Walk around, stretch. Keep everything moving. A far cry from the bed I had been placed in during the later stages of labour twenty-one years before. A long way off the missionary position they had made me adopt to give birth, passive and excruciatingly painful.

My birth plan is all in place – no intervention unless absolutely necessary, ideally no pain relief, not even gas-and-air if I can help it; from early on in the pregnancy I've attended yoga classes designed for 'easy' birth. This time *I* want to be the one in control. Me, Bert, and our baby, himself starting his long journey into the world. He too has a role to play in this drama.

By lunchtime I'm pretty sure these aren't more of the (by now) very familiar Braxton-Hicks, and then my waters break, as if to confirm we're ready for the off, about to meet our son – we know this baby is a boy - for the first time. This really is it. Anticipation and excitement are nudged out of the way by apprehension, then vice versa. My first experience of childbirth wasn't something I wanted to repeat. I pray to some nameless deity – probably female - that things will be different this time.

Mid-August, three days before my due date, and the sun shines gloriously from a kingfisher blue mid-day sky. Bert and I calmly walk up the road, so familiar and yet feeling so strange today, and around the corner to our regular local greengrocer.

"A couple of bananas, please."

We've read all the books and we know we need to keep our energies up – mine in particular, but we're aware this could be a marathon for Bert, too.

"When's that baby going to arrive? You've been pregnant for ever!" Tim places two sizeable spotted bananas on his weighing scales.

"Soon, I hope. I'm in labour."

"What the hell you doing here, then? Shouldn't you be in hospital or something!"

I explain things have changed since we were all born. Tim, in his fifties, is clearly unconvinced.

"Here, you have these on me. Now get off to that bloody hospital, girl!"

We've promised Helen we'll call her as soon as I go into labour, but she lives only a few hours away and to me it feels premature this early in the process. Based on my previous experience of childbirth, there's still some considerable time to go yet. We should wait and make sure this isn't another false alarm, I suggest; there is no hurry. (I hadn't, of course, thought about second births often being much quicker than first, but that was not to be an issue.) So we stroll calmly, joyously down Mill Road in the sun, and I'm full of excitement in contrast to the terror I'd felt twenty-one years ago - despite the odd twinge stopping me quite literally in my tracks.

By teatime Helen arrives, cooking dinner for all of us, and trying to finish the crib blanket she is in the middle of crocheting. The art takes me back to Granny's time, crochet having long become a very minority activity. The blanket's close to completion. The apricot, green and cream design won't, she knows, offend my sensibilities by gendering our baby in blue even before his birth. I smile that she is getting to know me a little, as I had always dreamed my daughter might.

"Don't be too quick, Sue. I need to finish this!" She has to be joking if she thinks I'm in control of anything here!

Early evening, and the contractions are strong, but when we ring the hospital they tell me they're still too far apart for me to be admitted. As I sprawl kneeling over an enormous Mister Men beanbag we've bought for the baby, my bump sinks into the middle and I practise the well-rehearsed breathing.

"Why not try a warm bath?" Bert suggests. It helped with period pains; maybe it would help with this, or at least move the labour on.

In the hot bubbly water I laugh aloud at not being able to see my toes beyond my gargantuan belly – I really am enormous. Bert takes a photo of me peering over the bump.

"Carrying lots of water," someone had said.

And my midwife? What had her verdict been?

"Carrying lots of baby."

Hmm.

"Will you rub my back, love?" I ask my deeply attentive partner. Unfortunately it's not me he's deeply attending to.

"Hang on a minute."

Anyone who knows him would be totally unsurprised to see Bert busy calculating moving averages of the gap between contractions to see if we're anywhere near heading for the hospital. With paper and pencil. To the third decimal point. Making frequent mistakes (must have been the pressure!) and corrections. I know exactly where I'd like to ram that pencil right now, but I just breathe through another surge and simultaneously provide him with another piece of data.

Amusing, yes. Eccentric, certainly. Frustrating, absolutely; and bloody annoying! Looking back, I can see what an omen that 'oh-so-practical exercise' of his was. To this day, Bert swears it was in my interest that he did those sums. Me? I now know he'll always feel less anxious at difficult times if he has a nice little bit of maths to cling onto. Maybe one day I'll even forgive him.

Another contraction.

"Let me." Helen soothes my pains with her tender touch.

By nine o'clock we're on our way to the hospital. Helen drives – Bert never has, except one occasion when the rest of his rock band on tour in Turkey in the seventies were all so stoned on acid that he had no choice but to take control of the van. The 'stuff', slipped into their palms during welcoming handshakes at an American airbase, was potent. "Good shit!" the others assured him, but he wouldn't touch it. At one point I myself had tried teaching him to drive when I was heavily pregnant, thinking this was 'a good idea'. It wasn't. The emergency stops nearly sent me into premature labour, and one or two other manoeuvres nearly caused me to wet myself. Pregnancy's like that.

Anyway, Helen drove us and there we are trying to gain access for my daughter to the birthing suite. She wants to be there when the baby's born.

"Are you family?" a nurse asks.

"I'm her daughter." It's the first time I've heard her say the words, the first time she will have done of course. Maybe it's my pregnant state, maybe it's my heightened emotions, but it knocks me sideways. I keep it to myself, as I'm so terribly used to doing, so very well-practised at when it comes to this young woman now standing beside me. We're told firmly it's one birthing partner only. Helen heads off home to a quiet, strange house – one holding its breath for the new baby's arrival. She finishes her baby brother's blanket that night while I labour.

The delivery ward is almost empty when we're checked in, so we have the luxury of a bathroom to ourselves for as long as we want or need. Once the first tests are done – monitoring our baby's heart rate, my blood pressure, getting me all labelled and measured for dilation (I was a pathetic seven centimetres) – I slide into that bath like a hippo on weed.

We've brought the Rutter Requiem (okay, admittedly an *odd* choice for a birth but I'd sung it with a choir in France and it brought back fond memories and a sense of tranquillity for the most part) and we've packed all the essentials of a birthing bag. We've prepared for most eventualities. But I'm not sure the midwife is or indeed could ever be fully prepared for Bert. A softly-spoken young woman who I'd swear isn't long out of nappies herself, our midwife is superb, exuding both confidence and competence, but with our approval leaving us to get on with things ourselves. These days birth is, it seems, a perfectly natural thing to be getting on with ourselves. How it has changed since 1972.

We both feel mighty relieved at being trusted to get on with this birth we feel we've prepared so well for, but even I am taken by surprise when Bert - determined to be as empathetic as he can - strips down to his underpants and almost gets in the bath beside me. (It's big enough. I still resist.) Leaning over the edge as my contractions swell, he strokes my arms tenderly, sweeping the tension down through my fingers and out again. And it seems to work, along with the rhythmic deep breathing - both him and me, that is. We're birthing our child together.

But with time rolling on the contractions are strengthening and I start to experience something I could never have imagined. Not one ever to have managed visualising candles and likewise to go off into a meditative trance, I'm thoroughly unprepared for what happens next. Along comes the strongest contraction so far, surging through the whole of my body like a fire touching every nerve and setting it alight.

"Look at me. Concentrate on breathing. Come on. Breathe in." He breathes with me, his capacious saxophonist's lungs filling in perfect time with my rather diminished efforts, my lungs squashed as they are by our baby.

"That's it. And out," he exhales.

And in that moment my eyes open into a clearing. I'm in a dark forest. In Africa somewhere, although how I know this is beyond me. I just do. Surrounding me is the blackest of black nights, and all around are tall torches, naked flames rising high, illuminating a circle of strong black women of all ages in vibrant African blouses, skirts and headscarves. Our hands are held tight as we stand in a ring, a powerful band of wise women. And with the tightening of the contraction the circle closes, drawing us women closer together, their power rising as their arms lift high above their heads, triumphant. And in that moment there is no pain, just a tightening of the circle, a focusing of power, a heralding of the birth that's soon to be. Holding it there, right there, arms aloft, hands holding tight...*tight*. And then the band releases its intense grip, falling back, the energy melting away. Their hands lower, breathing gentler, a shallow rise and fall of their breasts now and mine. One more breath and I'm back, eye to eye with Bert. Until the next contraction.

"Well done. You're doing great." He wipes the sweat from my brow.

"I've just been in Africa."

"That's nice, lovey."

He really is not on this planet.

"Press the bell if you need anything."

THAT PICTURE OF YOU

The same words. Twenty-one years later, the same words and yet such a different experience. This time I know we must call for help now, and this time I know I won't die. Our baby midwife is there as swift as an angel.

"Well done, you're doing really well. But I think it's time we get you out of this water."

Wishing I'd arranged a water birth I find myself in a delivery room, medical things waiting to ping and ding and sound alarms around me at any instant. But they don't. She checks our baby's heartbeat, my blood pressure, and we're both doing fine. And so we continue. I pace the room. I squat over bean bags and find all manner of positions to help. Bert reaches out to touch me. "Don't!" Suddenly my reaction is almost violent.

"What?" He's understandably bemused - there are one or two things he's forgotten about this birth process. So too have I. And his touch feels like nettles against my skin. I can't bear to have him near me. If he touches me I'll kill him! "Don't touch me!" The words fly out of my mouth and I know I mean them but they feel so wrong – and right!

"Great!" grins our midwife. "You're in second stage, Susan. Well done." I almost shout, "Don' call me Susan!" but manage to restrain myself.

Of course! I'd forgotten about this brief interlude where I'm *supposed* to feel like I could peel my partner's eyeballs out of his head. In this second stage something is surging through me with a vengeance.

"Oooh," I groan. "I need to push!" The urge is overwhelming.

"No, we're going to hold it right there," she tries to reassure. I'll take some convincing I'm hold anything anywhere, least of all this baby inside me.

"Right. Panting. Come on. We're not even thinking about the other P word. Just pant!" She is calm and firm.

"What can I do?" Bert's desperate to get this right. We've come so far as a team in this.

"Just get her to look at you and pant, Bert. Great! Well done. Easy now. Hold it there."

I look into Bert's eyes, and the urge to push is all-consuming. A groan escapes from somewhere so deep inside there are no words for this place. I'm sweating by the bucket. And little girl midwife is as cool as a lollipop.

"Yes. Great. Well done. Just keep that going. Pant, pant!"

And with what feels like one enormous rush…

"Oh, sweetheart!"

"Well done, Sue! You've birthed the baby's head!"

"I fucking well know I've birthed the baby's head!"

Not elegant. Not lady-like. But so, so true.

At 3.29 in the morning, a little before the sun rises on the fourteenth day of the eighth month, and two days earlier than expected Bert takes our beautiful, perfect baby boy in his arms. "Are you going to hold him?" he asks. And I'm filled with absolute terror that someone will take my baby away. I can't. I can't hold him. I'm terrified of the bond. "Look." Bert brings him up to my side. The baby's covered in mucous and blood, and is the most wonderful bundle of love.

"Look how beautiful our son is," he cries. "Aren't you clever!"

I am overwhelmed and exhausted but I hold out my arms and take our baby. He is *so* beautiful.

"Here," the midwife says, "he'd like to suck, I bet." And she shows me how to help my baby onto my breast. He latches on immediately. There is no other feeling in the world like this rush of maternal love. Against this all other things pale into insignificance.

Helen arrives around noon to drive us home. I feel there can be nothing more natural than the sight of her cradling our new-born, her brother, close to her breast. She of course looks the more likely mother of the two of us and Ben fits perfectly into her arms, swaddled in his baby green crib blanket. She hands him to me and I'm wheeled exhausted to the hospital door. This time no-one's carrying my baby out but me.

I sit in the back of the car holding him close – not one of us thought to bring a baby seat – and Helen takes the wheel. Bert is beside her.

"Sue," she calls maternally, "put your seatbelt on."

"I have," I reassure. She can't see that of course, but it doesn't matter one tiny bit. All she sees is my blue eyes meeting her green eyes in the rear-view mirror.

"Just make sure you hold that baby close," she says, her gaze fixed on me. "And never let go."

SUSAN J BEVAN

Postscript

As I write this, MAA (Movement for an Adoption Apology) is fighting for an apology from the British government for the way in which so many natural parents/birth mothers – call us what you will – were treated in decades gone by. Forced through social pressures to relinquish our children, the treatment of many young mothers was barbaric. I was incredibly lucky: I was sent to see out my pregnancy with a loving sister. Many of the half a million women in the UK who have lost a child to adoption were far less fortunate.

The Australian and Irish governments have both apologised for the role governments played in creating an environment in which young and often unmarried women were stigmatised into a situation which 'legitimised' removing their children from them, with no rights ever again to know if they were alive or dead. Even in my privileged position, I was never informed of any help there was for me to be able to keep my daughter and continue with my education and my life. 'Best for you, best for baby' was the mantra, with the clear subtext that I would be acting entirely selfishly and against my child's interest if I were even to think of challenging the official line. So I let my heart break, in silence and without a single counselling session and with no emotional support whatsoever, and as a fifteen-year-old I allowed my daughter - my first-born - to be raised by more 'respectable' parents.

I had hoped that by the time this book was to be published there would be progress towards an apology to the women who never even got to see their child – not even once in some case before they were taken; to the women whose children died in the care of adoptive parents without the birth mother even being told; to the mothers who have grieved and yearned and longed and suffered at the hands of a society that saw fit to deprive them of seeing their baby grow from girl child to woman, from boy to man. But I'm not holding my breath. I'm not breathing easy, but I'm not holding my breath.

In May 2012 MAA managed to get 92 MPs to sign an Early Day Motion to debate the government offering an apology for the things we suffered. This meant there was a possibility (albeit slim) of this being debated on the floor of The House of Commons. The problem is that very few of these motions ever get to debate. It was always going to be nothing short of a miracle if this one were to get there, particularly under the present government. But miracles happen. Every day little miracles happen, like when my daughter walked through my door on her twenty-first birthday.

But rather desperately for us birth parents this EDM, as all other EDMs, was timetabled to be removed altogether from the list exactly one year after being introduced, and that year will run out on May 21st 2013. After that, MAA would be back to the drawing board. So the picture as I wrote this book was bleak.

The wording of EDM 92 is:

That this House recognises the suffering that forced child adoptions during the 1950s, 1960s and 1970s caused, which took place due to social pressures on women who had children outside of marriage; notes the unacceptable adoption and care practices of the past, such as not giving information about welfare services including housing and financial help which were available at the time and not questioning whether women putting their children up for adoption had given informed consent; further recognises the negligence of previous Governments, with regard to ensuring that the care provided for unmarried mothers was appropriate and that they and their children were not mistreated or discriminated against, resulting in many women suffering traumatising pre and post-natal experiences and children being denied contact with their birth parents; and calls on the Government to apologise in order to go some way toward helping the parents and children who were victims of these practices.

But this gutsy and determined (and desperate) group of women has balls. Working with MPs and in particular the excellent John Leech, Liberal Democrat for Manchester Withington, they have produced a new Early Day Motion - EDM 77, introduced on May 14th 2013 and which is precisely the same as EDM 92 but ends thus:

...further notes that the Australian Prime Minister Julia Gillard has this year apologised to the victims of forced adoptions in Australia; and therefore calls on the UK Government to apologise in order to go some way toward helping the parents and children who were victims of these practices.

If you want to support this struggle for an apology, find MM here:

https://www.facebook.com/adoptionapology?fref=ts

Let's hope this succeeds, and brings a little closure to some of us.

And you know...'Sorry' costs nothing.

'Sorry' would be a start.

'Sorry' could be added to the picture, that picture of you.

Printed in Great Britain
by Amazon.co.uk, Ltd.,
Marston Gate.